The Happy Child

The Happy Child

Changing the Heart of Education

STEVEN HARRISON

SENTIENT PUBLICATIONS, LLC

Cover design by Kim Johansen, Black Dog Design
Book design by Bill Spahr

Library of Congress Cataloging-in-Publication Data

Harrison, Steven, 1954-
The happy child : changing the heart of education /
Steven Harrison.—
1st Sentient Publications ed.
p. cm.
ISBN 1-59181-000-0
1. Alternative education. 2. Education--Philosophy. I. Title.
LC46.3 .H37 2002
372.139—dc21   2002010861

ſENTIENT PUBLICATIONſ
A Limited Liability Company
1113 Spruce Street
Boulder, Colorado 80302
www.sentientpublications.com

Contents

Introduction

*In times of change, learners inherit the earth, while the
learned find themselves beautifully equipped to deal with a
world that no longer exists.*

　　　　　　　　　　　　　　　　—*Eric Hoffer*

I n all the discussion about how best to teach children, we don't
often hear about the purpose of education other than as a social obligation and the preparation of the child for the adult world
of work. We don't hear much about the child, and almost nothing *from* the child.

Perhaps all that education aspires to be is the preparation of
the young person for their role in the larger society. This is certainly a good idea for society, but in the efficiency of producing
citizen workers, are we missing the deeper meaning and higher
purpose of learning? Have we forgotten about the spirit of the
child, the unique and fragile expression of a passionate and integrated life?

This book is about a reorientation of education, a radical
and fundamental realignment of the purpose of education. Can
education shift from its current model of shaping children into
components of economic production, into an active experiment
in optimizing the creativity of the whole child? We have been
so busy educating our children that we have missed the heart of
education, the creation of a happy life. A happy life, after all, is

not only what we would like for our children, but for ourselves as well.

A happy person, fulfilled in their connection to their friends, family, and community and in the expression of their vocation, is likely to be useful and productive in their life and to help weave the collective fabric of a functional society. What else should a society need from education other than the happiness of its people? What else should we demand for our children other than their happiness?

Perhaps we are a little afraid of happiness. We were educated from that state long ago, molded into a set of skills and a catalog of information. Our education was not to fulfill us, but to fulfill the needs of productivity in the marketplace. But children are born knowing all about the creative life, and fortunately, creativity is hereditary—we can easily inherit it from our children!

In this book you will find sparse reference to studies of children's behaviors or the research on their learning. There are no citations and only passing reference to expert theory on education. While this book explores raising and educating happy children, it is written with the premise that children have an innate capacity for happiness and for learning that has become more and more obstructed by the plethora of experts and their theories. This book is an attempt to explore the possibilities of letting children grow into adulthood in relationship to their parents, peers, family, and community, but without the interference of the mechanical and stultifying conditioning we now call education. In the end, we must address the whole of life in order to educate the whole child.

While I may often discuss children and their creativity and expression in the pages that follow, I am not writing this book for children. They do not need this book, or any book, on how to learn. But for parents, caretakers, teachers, and adults who care about children, there is a great challenge to trust children to learn at their own pace, in their own way, and under the conditions of their choosing. Perhaps, too, this is written for those young people who are no longer children but are beginning to forge their own way in life, yet who carry the burden of the false education to which they have been subjected.

This book grew out of the deep explorations and discussions that occurred in the founding of a learning community—The Living School in Boulder, Colorado. In facing the complex questions of child rearing, education, autonomy and relatedness, and the fragmentation of society, it was obvious that no matter what we had come to understand, no matter what the admirable models of alternative education from Waldorf to Summerhill we could find, the challenge that we were facing to create a living, learning community would take us into uncharted territory. At first this was disorienting and there was pressure to congeal the investigation into a solid philosophy. But soon enough there was the exhilarating realization that the recognition of unknowing is in fact the very quality we are trying to embody in the learning environment we are determined to provide for the children of our community.

Unknowing is the expression of the driving curiosity that we see in the children around us. They are completely comfortable in a state of continuous learning, where we as adults often seek conclusion. There is no conclusion to a learning community and there is no beginning point.

While there may be a building called a school, this is really not the soul of the learning community. Rather, the essence of the learning community is the recognition that we can all, young and old, share the open investigation of our world in whatever way and with whatever capacity we have. That relationship of open learning also happens to be a relationship of great happiness.

So many of us involved with children are deeply dissatisfied with schools in our society. Many more of us are not so much unhappy with those schools as numb to them. After all, most of us went through those same schools and understand them as the only way education takes place. It is not in the parents and adults that we will see the indicators of what is wrong, or what needs to happen, but in the children, who begin their lives with such an explosion of interest in learning and creativity of expression and who, after years of education, emerge as adults so much stripped of those same qualities.

We can easily imagine a different possibility—one in which the natural curiosity and love of life that we begin with carries through into our adult years. We have the innate capacity as human beings to embrace and relate to all of life just as it is and at the same time to transform it through the creativity that comes so naturally out of that openness, attention, and empathy. We birth children who have this capacity; what if we let them live in that all of their lives? What if we trust this movement of life, embodied in the child, to develop and express an entirely different way of living? What if we offer them the safety and security of our strength and our knowledge of the world without the demand that they understand life in the same way that we do? What if we give them the freedom, respect, and responsibility commensurate with their actual capacity? What if we joined in the endless passion of a life of learning and relationship?

In a world with immense and complex challenges, we can say with certainty that we have come up with no clear answers. We have working hypotheses, holding actions, band-aids, and many excuses, but we have no resolution to the problems of our world. We do have a resource that we have barely touched upon and it is remarkable that we have managed to almost totally suppress it in our public institutions and governing bodies. We have the human potential for immensely creative and transformative approaches to life's challenges, new forms of living and being that thrive in the mind of imagination and the holistic considerations of consciousness. If there are solutions, they will be found in the unfettered, undivided expression of the connected, heartfelt, conscious human being—the happy child grown into the integral intelligence of an adult whose inner and outer expression are one, whose mind is mastered, but not the master, and whose individuation is connected to all of life.

The Happy Child

Learning and Happiness

A little boy came home from school and complained to his mother, "I'm not going back tomorrow. I can't read yet. I can't write. And they won't let me talk."

A book on the happy child would be short indeed if happy adults populated our world. A child finds happiness naturally, but also finds every other quality just as fluidly. Surrounded by pressures and conflicts, the child easily takes on those patterns. Any discussion of the happiness of a child must turn eventually to the world that the child inhabits; any solution to education must address the adults who create the conditions in which learning takes place.

The child is built to be what the child is. This seems like an unnecessary and self-defining statement. But, the common view is that children are to be molded, trained, educated. In this view, children do not have an inherent life force that deserves the respect we accord to the adult population.

We are concerned to the degree of obsession with what we will make of our children and begin engineering them at an increasingly early age. Not content with school at six years of age, we have continued the logical regression into preschools, early learning, infant education, pre-natal music, ultra-sound screening, and pre-marital genetic counseling. We are certain we will create the perfect child through all of this, but would we recognize perfection if we finally came upon it through all of our manipulation? Is perfection a mini-me—a driven, productive homunculus? Or is it possible that perfection is simply what the child is, just as he or she is? Doesn't the child, like the adult, hold the essential, existential quandary of synthesizing the whirl of thought, feeling, and action into a meaningful life?

This is an important exploration that will color all of our views of educating our children. For those who see the child as born failed and broken, in need of repair and redirection, education will mean a revamping of the child that is, into the child that should be. For the more sophisticated parent, the child, while not broken, needs the enlightenment of implanted values, specifically the parental values.

We are all adults who "should be," and we are never enough of whatever that is. We can easily implant this essential dissatisfaction in our children and induct them into the cult of unhappiness that looks to materialism for its solace.

But if we don't see children as broken at birth, then what are they if not a mystery? Can we join with them in exploring the unknown of their life and have the strength to reveal to them that we live in the unknown too? In that, we are not trying to change them, or ourselves for that matter, but rather we are reveling in the amazing discoveries that life holds for all of us. We cannot teach our children to drink deeply of life because the knowledge of life is not transferred by will. But children can understand so easily if they are not stopped, more so if they see that the adults in their life are continuously learning.

The question of the happy child turns to the question of the happy adult. Where is happiness to be found for either other than in their shared and playful life journey of open exploration?

Educating the Whole Child

*If (man) thinks of the totality as constituted of independent
fragments, then that is how his mind will tend to operate, but
if he can include everything coherently and harmoniously
in an overall whole that is undivided, unbroken, and without
a border then his mind will tend to move in a similar way,
and from this will flow an orderly action within the whole.*

—David Bohm

What does it mean to educate the whole child? This should be an easy question. We should be able to learn about the whole child by looking at what the whole child is a part of: a whole parent, a whole family, and a whole society. But, unfortunately, we don't find many whole parents, whole families, and whole societies. All of these tend to be fractured, dysfunctional, and confused. Our challenge is to find a way to interact with each child that enables the child to develop in wholeness even in a fragmented world.

Education systems presume that children need to be fixed, but are they broken? Are they not already expressing what we say we want to get from our education system—curiosity, creativity, and communication? Are they not already building skills, acquiring information, and effectively socializing at a pace that far exceeds the adults?

When we consider the possibility of educating the whole child, we must consider all of the dimensions of the human being, not simply the intellectual. We can't say that expanding the education to include verbal, mathematical, and graphic learning will describe the whole child. We can say we want to educate the intellectual, emotional, physical, and even the spiritual elements of the child, and this still will not describe the whole child. We need to recognize the unfathomable, prewired, genetic disposition of the child along with the apparent plasticity of the brain in its response to the environment. We need to educate the child-in-relationship, the collection of attributes that the child is, as well as the way that the child interacts with the world and the way the world responds.

The whole child is the epicenter of a web of multi-directional communications and responses. Teaching the child to simply objectify and quantify the complexity of life is also teaching a reduction in capacity, rather than an embrace of the full human capacity. This reduction in the guise of education may well have been a functional response to a bygone era, but it is hardly the challenge of the contemporary day. Today there is tremendous utility in understanding the interrelatedness of organizational systems on all levels, from managing a corporate work group to facing the issue of global ecological imbalance. A fragmented education will no longer serve the increasing need to understand the management of the unprecedented lightning speed of the flow of information, world cultural collision, and diminishing resources from oil to water. Nor does the education of anything less than the whole child serve the child.

The education system that we have in place now came out of the transition from the agrarian society to the industrial society. Our education system was a way of preparing agricultural workers for jobs in industry. The great narrative, the story that we tell ourselves about public education, is that if our child is educated, he or she will be able to be successful. It is through education that our children will have a piece of the economic action. If you leave the farm, if you go to the city, there are jobs, there are resources that will be yours.

There were other tradeoffs, of course—the relative independence and self-sufficiency of the farm was given up for the employment dependence of the urban economy, but also the harder life of the farm was exchanged for the relative comforts of the urban and suburban life. Large-scale public education helped with this transition.

Our education system, like our economy, is set up to create a product. The product is a worker in industry. This is its historic purpose, and whether it was truly educating the populace or simply conditioning the individual to become subservient, public education did create a workforce that drove an unprecedented economic machine over the past century.

But is this system producing a worker for the post-modern information age or is it producing a vestigial, useless remainder from the past? Is an industrial worker what we need at this point, or does something else need to be engendered by our education system?

On a practical level, is a person who is taught not to think, but to jam information in and push information out, valued in our contemporary society? The children we are teaching today will be in their adulthood in a decade or two. In that world, the world of twenty years from now, will a child who has been filled with information—not even contemporary information, but information from a decade or two ago—be skilled, functional, prized? Will a child who has learned to hold and regurgitate information be esteemed? It is obvious that the computers will be doing it better, that the computers are already pushing information in and out better than most of us. It is not information that will be useful, but the ability to understand how to utilize it.

Looking down the road to our children's future, what will be far more important than yesterday's factoids is the relationship our children will have to the then-existing systems of information. A child who is given the chance to explore and investigate the sources of information, the meaning of information, the utility of information, and the skills of manipulating and crafting information will be able to move fluidly in this future.

The irony is obvious. Children explore information in this way naturally and are interrupted only by the harshest of measures: being taken to schools, made to sit still, made to stop talking, made to listen and remember bits of information. Information in, information out, just like a computer. Of course, computers do it faster, with greater accuracy, and without sleep, lunch breaks, or vacations.

Fortunately, something about the wholeness of a child is different from a computer, different than just the capacity to hold information. Human intelligence is integral. It can look at the bits of information and understand the relationship. But, are we teaching that? Is that what is learned in school when a twelve-year-old sits only with other twelve-year-olds learning only geometry for the state required tests for exactly fifty minutes until the bell rings? Is that child learning the interrelationship of everything or is he learning information separated from everything else? Are we teaching an intelligence relating all the systems of a human being or are we teaching a limited range of primarily intellectual areas? Is it any wonder that children often feel disconnected? We are teaching them disconnection, valuing one small area of the human faculties over all others.

Let us model a different kind of possibility: children as whole, not yet finished in their development, but fluidly moving through their thoughts and feelings, exploring their inner and outer capacities, acutely aware of the social systems in which they live. Let us give them a supportive environment, the freedom to express themselves, and the responsibility for their learning. Let us give them educational communities in which the students direct their own learning without coercion, threat, or convincing; where interest, not compulsion, brings them to attend; where they have the responsibility for their learning and the freedom that grows naturally with that responsibility. Further, let us join them fully in the exploration of the whole of life, because without our complete participation their journey will be burdened by the debris of our fear.

Children have the ability to state their educational needs if we don't take that ability away from them by our sheer size, by intimidation, and by the implicit threat of violence. If we do let them direct their learning, the element of self-direction is in and of itself a dimension of education that will never take place in the current school environment of force-feeding information to passive students.

It is easy to see the ability to self-direct learning with a very young child, but when children get a little older, they not only have the will, but they start to develop the intellect to challenge us, and then it's time for the big yellow school bus to come and take them away.

Many parents are willing to simply send their kids off someplace. And the parents, of course, go off to someplace else, and never the twain shall meet. It is a mystery where the children disappear to, and where the parents disappear to, and for that matter, what's happening at their home while they're all gone.

The idea of shipping our children off to a warehouse where they are educated by strangers from a curriculum designed by politicians and academic theorists is so strange and disconnected from the reality of a child that we have to wonder how this could come to be the fact in our society. Why would we want our children treated like this? Only by being convinced that it is for their own good—or if we don't happen to agree, by being subject to fines and imprisonment if we don't comply—would we go along with this. After all, we allow ourselves to be sent off, indeed we transport ourselves to be warehoused at work, so we can imagine such a fate would be acceptable to our children.

The world that we live in has this kind of fragmentation to it. We are fragmented: our workplaces, our schools, our society. Yet, we must find a way to raise a whole child, one who can meet the future fully, without fear, with an intelligence that can understand and move in new and challenging situations.

The child needs our love, our support, and the demonstration of our wisdom through the way we live our lives, the way we work, the way we form our communities. We cannot hope to be useful to these children without first understanding our own fragmentation. Perhaps we were children sent off on the yellow school bus to learn facts and figures, to be rewarded and punished, tested, socialized. How are we—the results of a disconnected education—going to guide a child through an integral education? Do we even recall, because of our own education, what wholeness is in our experience?

Until the child is emancipated at the age of eighteen, the parents provide the basic material needs. That's our contract because we begat a child, we took on the custodianship of a child, or we have a relationship with a child, so we are going to take care of a child in the material ways—food, clothing, and shelter. Beyond that, do school-aged children need us to impose ourselves as mediators of their experience?

We want the best for our children. We want to protect them from failure and harm. We want to increase their chances of happiness and success. How will we know what to do for them?

It is often noted that there should be a support group for the children of gifted parents. If I am a gifted parent I will project onto my child that this is a gifted child who is going to be just like me and will want everything that I always wanted. Those of us who are parents are no doubt all gifted parents! So let's start violin lessons because the child is three years old and this will give him an early start. That sort of imposition of all the things that I have accomplished, and often all the things I never accomplished, begins to form a neurotic relationship to the child.

We might wonder how a child knows a violin even exists without being exposed to it? Having a violin around is not an imposition. Leaving it around with music and a violin teacher every Thursday at 3 o'clock while tapping your foot, waiting for interest to occur, could be. The expectation translates into pressure. The child does not discover the violin—only the parents' expectations.

Non-coercive learning takes place in an environment that is responsive to the child and in which the child is informed factually, but without a particular learning direction implied. Children are interactive; they communicate and take in communication constantly. The simple act of open listening and the honest, direct response that neither strips the child of responsibility nor imposes authority actualizes the potential of the whole child. What is taught is not so much the information, the concept, or the skill, as much as the demonstration of interaction from the common ground of relationship. This, as it turns out, is quite a lot and quite enough.

Learning to Fail

When childhood dies, its corpses are called adults and they enter society, one of the politer names of hell. That is why we dread children, even if we love them, they show us the state of our decay.

— *Brian Aldiss*

Failure is not only an intrinsic part of success; it is often richer in opportunities for learning than the experience of accomplishment. We don't typically get to success without failure, so our relationship to failure is a defining aspect of our life.

Where does our idea of personal failure come from? Look directly to your own experience to discover the source of the message of your shortcomings—the voices of those who told you that you were good or bad, right or wrong, your own voice that tells you that you are not good enough. Here we can begin to see the importance of letting a child develop his or her own sense of failure and success, of value, meaning, and interest.

From an early age we reward our children with praise, often contrived, to motivate them to continue acting in certain ways.

Equally confusing, we often withdraw our emotional support when their exploration of life takes them into behaviors we don't like. A child can understand fairly quickly what the adult thinks about the child's actions. This is not what is confusing. The child learns that we like them to draw on the paper and not the wall. Later they learn that we like or don't like their clothes, music, friends, manners, and so forth. This is not confusing at all. What is confusing for many children is that they are never given a chance to figure out what *they* like and don't like, what draws their passion and energy into complete engagement. Children are often not given the chance to find out what failure means to them, and so they may never know the meaning of success.

Ironically, it may be the high achievers who can understand their success and failure only in terms of externals: grades, jobs, and income. Those who are a success at understanding the pathways to external rewards may never learn what is intrinsically rewarding. Being skilled at collecting external rewards may have nothing to do with happiness. Those children who experience failures have the chance to look at what intrinsic qualities make them happy, since they are not finding it in the external rewards. Why should a child have to sift through a predefined sense of success and failure, or external reward and punishment, to understand the nature of a joyful life?

Children, if left to explore, can discover their passions—the activities, the skills that bring forth the totality of their life energy in an engaged, full-tilt expression that is creative, productive, and not coincidently—happy. What an amazing concept—happy children! Why do we interfere with this? Why do we think that we need to redirect other beings' unmediated connection to their own hearts? Of course they are children, so we can do that if we like.

We are bigger, stronger, and know the pathways of power far better than they do. But why do we want to take passionate children and make them into adults looking for happiness?

Without the interference of powerful adults who define success and failure and who set child against child in competition for the rewards of attention, praise, and status, failure takes on a different meaning to a child. The response in the child's environment is just a part of the expression of failure—only one component in balance with the inner considerations, the creative soul of the child's drive to understand.

For the passionate child, failure is not something imposed just from the outside, but something that connects the inner drive and the outer response, and observes the totality of it. Perhaps it is the external that defines the failure: a chemistry experiment gone wrong, a painting no one understands, a social advance rejected. Perhaps the failure is internal: the loss of interest in a project, the inability to master a musical instrument or to find a full expression in a poem. But this failure is not defeat; it has no demand that behavior change or a particular result be achieved. The exploration of failure for the child is the investigation of what the child is. It is the sorting of the interests, learned skills, and intrinsic abilities into a life. It is inextricably linked to success—authentic success as an integrated human being, not just a bundle of acceptable behaviors. Each child, each person, has the deep need to find this integration both in themselves and in relationship to the world around. When this fundamental need is thwarted, the destruction of the soul leaves an intact shell of compromised personality, but an empty heart.

As children, we adults may not have been given the chance to explore our heartfelt expression. We learned to obey or disobey;

we developed our social persona relative to the rewards and punishments of the educational and parenting styles of the day. Now, as we sort through the debris of our life expressions to find the slivers of our shattered heart, we can do one simple thing. We can give the children of this day the chance to find their heart intact, to find its expression and live that expression. We can give these children the chance to fail and succeed on their own terms, to measure the internal and external response to their passion. This is the possibility of the healing of our broken hearts; it is the transformation of fragments into the whole. This simple act—allowing our children to be—will change the heart of education.

Who is the Educator?

Three educators were walking in the woods when they came to some tracks. "These are from deer," said the first. "No, most certainly elk," said the second. "I am sure it is moose," said the third. They were still arguing when the train hit them.

M any educators have studied how children learn, or studied with those who studied how children learn, or at least studied in classes on educational theory various speculations of how children learn. Only the innovators, the rebels, the visionaries have stepped out of theory into the lives of children to ask the children how they learn or what learning is for a child. For most educators, contact with children and learning comes *after* the educator has learned how to teach and only after many years of being taught how to learn (which by inference is how to teach).

It is little wonder that innovation in education is difficult to find. Education theory—the result of mainstream education and its underlying assumptions—can hardly formulate something entirely new, fresh, and fundamentally different. Teaching technology is fixed in its self-perpetuation. Innovation, experimentation, and inquiry—the very essence of learning—are not part of the repertoire of institutionalized education. Through the agendas of academic institutions, corporate funding, educational publishers and consultants, and political pressures, schools have become an amalgam of social engineering and crass manipulation with children as the guinea pigs. The results are staggeringly awful, not just in declining literacy and general competence of young people, but also in the increasing violence growing out of the failure that is contemporary education. Unlike most businesses, in which such results would mean the end of the firm, the education business—a multi-billion-dollar enterprise—grows by creating continuous fixes for its own ineptitude.

Parents are often oblivious to the odd, sometimes crackpot theories behind the educational programs to which their child is subjected. Some parents take the time to understand the education systems and attempt to make reasoned choices on behalf of their children. But this reasoning often disregards the parents' attention to their own fears and anxieties about what they want for their child. Without the parents' understanding of these projections, the child becomes a proxy for the parents' unfulfilled dreams. The earlier these dreams are realized, the better. Even babies should be learning: the Mozart Effect in the crib, Baby Einstein videos when they wake, and if they can't sleep after their educational day, the Farber Method will help the parents ignore their child's cries until they have exhausted themselves. This is the parents' drive to perfection, the pressure to achieve, the competition for resources, the fear that my child won't make it, that I won't make it.

A pressured babyhood becomes an overscheduled, over-achieving, and pressurized childhood. Is it any surprise that children are blowing up, breaking down, tuning out, withdrawing, measuring their worth by their test scores and designer jeans, and communicating through pagers, cell phones, and instant messaging in order to hook up for drive-by relationships, drive-through food, and driven lives? This is what they learned at school and at home. What they learned was to be faster and better, or more precisely, that they were not fast enough or good enough. Some learned to run harder, some learned to give up. A very few children, endowed with an unusual measure of common sense and innate trust in themselves, learned that they are just fine, as they are, whatever they are. These few children were lucky to be slow learners, that is, they never learned the way they were supposed to learn, just the way they naturally learned.

How does the learning process look from the child's vantage? The child's perspective has nothing to do with collecting a body of knowledge, per se. Learning is the consequence of exploration driven by curiosity. Information is collected, not as a commodity in itself, but as an adjunct to the process. Information is a tool that is utilized as necessary to continue the investigation.

Curiosity has an enigmatic quality. It is difficult to create in a child, but easy to destroy. Young children are interested in areas we have long forgotten are even there. They are fascinated by how common objects are put together and what is inside those objects. Most adults don't concern themselves with what the inside of a telephone looks like, but a young child will expend a great deal of time and energy taking such a common object apart, looking at it, and playing with the pieces.

In the same way, children are endlessly interested in how they interact with the world around them and how that world responds. They are acutely aware of the power structures and how to influence them. This social intelligence also makes children particularly alert to the underlying purpose of adults and adept at responding appropriately to influence adults. This obscures many ill-considered learning environments where it would seem that a teacher is teaching children some body of information, where in fact the children are behaving strategically in relation to the adult and the power that adult wields. Even in such a situation, curiosity drives the child as the exploration continues—what happens if I cooperate, what happens if I don't, if I answer correctly, if I don't, and so forth?

The teacher is often so enraptured with the mission of conveying information that the pedagogical obsession becomes the defining purpose of the relationship to the child. The child, understanding this, responds accordingly, and discovers the pathways to success with the teacher—the subject matter becoming a sideline to the whole affair.

The subject matter of the teacher is likely not to engage the child in the least. And why should it? Most subjects are so abstracted and distant from a child's life and interests that it would seem odd if even the slightest interest were there.

We religiously teach letters to young children, always happy that they can parrot back the names. But to children of this age, the name of a letter may have no meaning other than that the parent or teacher seems particularly interested in the letters and very happy when the child is also. So the child is "interested," which means for the child, pleasing to the parent or authority.

We have to reward these children with exclamations of their goodness and brilliance when they say their letters or the name of some object or later can read that name. We don't consider the perspective of the child, who may worry about the withdrawal of our affection if the child doesn't know, or worse, really doesn't care.

Of course, children are curious about letters and numbers and reading. But we don't know much about what they experience in this regard. A letter may be an interesting shape, a transmission from some other dimension of sound, an entity that lives with fullness connected to so many other objects (A is for apple), or the means to hold the mind/hand in a fascinating dance of creativity and reproduction. For a child a letter could be so many things, but for the adult a letter is simply part of the symbol system out of which we construct the written word. The rest of the child's experience seems not very important, so long as the child can recognize, say, and write the symbol. Later it becomes important just that the child can read and write groups of letters as words.

As the children learn, they learn what the teacher thinks is important, and so letters become just letters, part of the symbol system called words. Later they will learn that learning fast is good, that being right is important, that some kids are smarter than others (the others are dumber), that suppression of feeling and expression of thought (at least certain thoughts) is valued. Or perhaps, such a child will grow up in a more progressive atmosphere where disregard for the obvious differences between kids is considered right, where group dynamics are reinforced and individual initiative is downplayed, where cool feelings are valued over hot ones, where the suppression of bad thoughts and the cultivation of good thoughts is imbedded in the culture. Or the child grows up in a hodgepodge of valued and distained behaviors. The successful child learns the drill, adopts the valued behaviors. The failed child learns to behave in ways that just are not acceptable, perhaps because there aren't any successful positions available or because the child cannot modify the natural tendencies so thoroughly. Both kinds of children have learned and both kinds have found their places through the behaviors they have taken on.

How many educators observe this macro-learning phenomenon? Do they see that the subject matter may be largely irrelevant other than as a means to achieve success or failure in the social structure created by the school? All teachers, regardless of the subjects they think they are teaching, are really teaching the same thing: relationship. Children really want to know about each other and socializing seems the main reason kids put up with the challenges of school.

In the beginning, perhaps they looked to their teachers to find out something about relationship, but too many teachers droned on about geography or long division. Eventually kids give up on adults for meaningful clues to relationship and turn to each other to figure it out. Often it is too late; the patterning is already etched and the patterns are simply played out child to child—the painful and destructive patterns learned at the feet of the masters: the teachers and the parents.

But regardless of the patterning of the child, the reality is that other children become the predominant source of interaction, socialization, information and, in fact, education. Yet this resource is wasted because we restrict the interaction between children while they are in school. Talking to each other is treated like it is aberrant behavior when it is the most natural of human expressions and a defining element of the species. Children are segregated by age, leaving the most obvious mentors—that is, older children—without the admiration from and the responsibility for the younger children. Children have a relationship to each other, regardless of their ages, and we have taught them to shut that off in the bizarre form of coercion called a classroom. In doing so, we have lost a huge and potent population of dynamic, inspired, and effective teachers—the children themselves.

Children learn from what is of interest to them, what is in their immediate world, what is in relationship to what they are.

Who is the educator? Education is in the whole, not just in the teacher. The child does not miss anything; the parents, the community, the school, the teacher, and the peers are all part of the whole, are all the educators. What the child learns is what is in the totality of the child's life, the inner and the outer. When the teacher steps into the totality of that life, from the totality of the teacher's life, and each completely engages the other in the passion of learning something of deep interest, education occurs because learners are present—the educator is no where to be found.

Education and Fear

Learning without Fear

A little boy came home from school with a note from the
teacher saying he doesn't have an inquiring mind. The
mother, of course, was quite upset by the note.

"You need to have an inquiring mind. I'm going to make
you have an inquiring mind. If I have to keep you studying
around the clock, you'll have an inquiring mind," said the
mother.

The boy asked, "What's an inquiring mind?"
"Oh, don't ask so many questions!"

L earning has something to do with experiencing a novel situation, assimilating the nature of the experience, and understanding its embedded information. We cannot learn in an
integral way without all of these aspects woven together.

We could come across something new without learning anything about it. We could certainly gather information or technology without the essential experience. But learning fragments of
an experience is not the essential learning of the experience itself.

Integral learning is whole in its nature, complete in the
absorption of what is new into the knowledge and technology
of it. Partial learning—the learning of some part of the whole—

is deluded at best, and at worst, dangerous if not recognized as fragmented.

The history of learning, the history of knowledge, is replete with the carnage of incomplete learning masquerading as fact. The cult of knowledge has only on occasion cracked under the weight of avoiding what it does not know.

As a culture enamored with technology, it is has been our tendency to embrace the doing part of learning, since this leads to greater productivity. Education has come to overemphasize learning technology and information at the expense of both the essential comprehension and the integration of the experience.

Businesses can produce goods and services incredibly efficiently without the slightest notion of what is being done or why, rarely introspecting on its higher purpose. Scientific research, driven by the forces of economics and academia, seldom steps back from itself to check on its connection to life around it. Educators, mired in the same market forces, direct their students as if productivity was the totality of human experience and the good of the state its highest temple.

We don't know a lot about learning because we have typically learned from a place of fear. What we have ended up learning a great deal about is survival.

At school we learned that the right answer was good, the wrong answer was bad, and if we had the right answer we could sit in the front row, if we didn't have the right answer we'd better sit back somewhere where we could hide out.

More insidiously, we learned that there was a right answer. We were taught that and we believed it. The problem with right answers is that it means there are a lot of wrong answers. The chances of having a wrong answer are far higher than of having the right answer, and so many of us understood we'd better hide out since the chances were we were wrong.

This whole idea of right and wrong answers is a bit absurd, looking back now, but at the time it seemed quite plausible. It seems reasonable enough that information is static and that once you know it, you know something. It is no doubt true that you know something, but the utility of that something frequently decays rather rapidly. I learned how to use a slide rule, that nuclear energy was the clean alternative to coal, that the Soviet Union existed, and so many other facts and skills that I got right, but which are currently wrong, questionable, useless, or non-existent.

How is it that fear motivates learning? When we encounter a new circumstance, we don't know exactly what it is and so we have to learn about it. If we learn about it through fear, perhaps we will survive. We can figure out a safe way to move through the situation, to listen or respond, and to leave intact. We model what's going to take place in that situation based on what we already know. If I know the answer that the teacher is asking for, then I'll raise my hand. If I don't know the answer, I won't raise my hand. If I know what happens in a situation, I'll take more risks.

Why is it that we learn out of fear instead of curiosity? We could come into a new situation and we could be immensely interested in it. We could be fearless and engaged. We could make contact with every aspect of what we encounter. Why is it that we go with fear, rather than curiosity? Why are we interested in educating our children to live in that same way?

A young child is not yet indoctrinated and will learn through curiosity, by finding out what a situation is by sampling it directly, by fearlessly making mistakes. Children have to learn that there's something called "wrong." From their perspective—where wrong doesn't exist as psychological failure—there's a 100 percent chance that they'll be right, even when they are totally wrong. Every answer that they come up with is a possibility, every experience that they come up with is a valid experience, and they're learning. They're learning about everything.

Is it possible to educate a child by letting that natural curiosity, that fearlessness, the ability to go into new situations and make full contact, lead the way? Or do we need to create in them the safety that comes along with fear? This is the safety that we have learned, to be afraid and to function from that fear. This is a fundamental question that we have to face as human beings, as members of our society, and as parents. Do we live from fear or do we live with the inherent risk of exploration? Do we live from separation and safety or do we live from contact? We can make this question an intellectual question about our children, about educational theory or philosophy of life. Or we can make this a deep question about ourselves and how we are living, how we are raising our children, and how we are creating our culture, which is in the end what we will bestow to those who are now young.

Failing Grades

One had to cram all this stuff into one's mind for the examinations, whether one liked it or not. This coercion had such a deterring effect [upon me] that, after I had passed the final examination, I found the consideration of any scientific problems distasteful to me for an entire year.

—Albert Einstein

Fear is often the measurement of how we are doing relative to each other, not as friends, colleagues, or members of community, but as competitors. That is embodied in schools by grading students. "A" people are doing better than "B" people who are doing better than "C" people.

Each of us qualifies what is taking place in our life. We compare it to other experiences. What happened before and what is happening now become the grade that we're giving this experience. We like it or dislike it. It evokes fear or pleasure. We grade our experiences. We compare this experience to that experience, the past to the present. We compare the first grader in this class to the first grader in that class. This is the structure of our world.

What is it that doesn't have a grade or a qualification to it? What in our experience, our life, our culture, or our schools has a richness to it that draws us in, requires us to investigate by making deeper and deeper contact? We could call this quality curiosity. We could call it passion. It is a compelling force in all of our lives. It informs us of what is in our heart and it has no grade, no qualification, no judgment.

It seems absurd to take the experience of learning, which is essentially driven by curiosity, and have it qualified by an external arbiter. But this is the fact of our schools and it is the reality of the structure of power in these places that it is the teacher who assigns the grades, not the learner. The educational marketplace is funny in that way—a coerced market in which the manufacturer judges the consumer, rather than a free market where shoddy products have no customers.

We have structured education with certain areas valued. In our public schools, mathematics and writing skills may be far more important than music, art, or the wildly aberrant act of just sitting quietly, contemplating, dreaming. There is going to be a math class in every single semester of every single school because it's valued so highly. There's not going to be a woodworking class in every single semester. There's not going to be a class on philosophy. There surely will not be a class on education; we are too busy educating to ever considering the nature of education itself.

Who is setting the agenda of valuation, and what happens to those who don't get to be in the category that is highly valued? What we actually are saying is, "The quality that you hold isn't valuable; the value that I will teach you is. And if you're good at learning the particulars of what I'm teaching you, then you'll become valuable. If not, you will be discarded."

Grades are codes that tell us all of this and more. We accept this intellectual profiling because it efficiently culls the less able from those with high capacity. This helps us organize the social structures of our society. If you like the social structures of a highly competitive society, you probably love grades. The idea is simple. A small percentage is at the top. A large percentage is in the middle. And there are the rest, the failures, at the bottom. This is the curve—a statistical distribution of grades that consistently and flawlessly produces a few winners, a lot of also-rans, and some losers. Tinkering social engineers and academic Brahmins created the system and gave themselves an A for arbitrary, when they might have gotten an F for fallacious, if anyone had been paying attention.

There is another possibility: that we value children just as they are and give them the responsibility to direct their own learning and to evaluate it in intrinsic terms. Mastery of an area might be presented to others to verify that understanding. We all like to find out from time to time how we are doing. If a self-directed learner wants to enroll in a college, then there are many demonstrations of understanding that might be required, including competitive testing. The motivation to proceed in that direction will also be the motivation to prepare for the entrance requirements.

When you remove the forced, repetitive evaluations, the spirit of learning is not broken in the learner who is paced more slowly, or whose interests deviate. Removing grades returns the freedom to learn to the individual, who no longer must take in and put out information on command to earn a reward.

Learning takes place in the freedom to encounter something, to have the full experience of that contact, to have the space to integrate that experience, and to have the time to learn the technology of that experience (what its characteristics are and how to utilize them). Learning is unimaginably complex and beautiful.

The experience is entirely different when you are being told what your experience is, the explanation of that experience, and what you can and cannot do with it. It is dead to the learner because it is only the representation of the experience as information without the complexity, the allure, the sparkle of full-dimension, engaged, and self-motivated learning. Information can be graded; sparkle cannot.

When we are handed the experience as a concept to be remembered, there is only the technological or functional relationship to it, without any integration. From a productivity standpoint, this is all that schools need to do. Workers don't need soul, only functional learning. It is obvious that there is an important difference between complex and active learning and rote conceptual intake, but that importance is only to the child, not the society.

Isn't it important that each student fit into society? So what if some teacher says I can't draw purple horses? I'll get over it, won't I? I won't be an artist and I'll learn to be an engineer. Perhaps society needs engineers more than it needs pictures of purple horses. Even if I hate engineering and I am just doing it for the money, I can go home at night and paint my horses. Society needs bridges, computers, and machines.

Is society more important than the actualization of the individual? Can a society have a soul when its citizens have been stripped of theirs by design, by force, by schools?

You certainly couldn't have everyone actualized, because you'd have a lot of poets and painters. Happy people don't necessarily want to work. You have to have a system that allows a certain percentage to be at the top and a certain percentage to be below so that someone is assembling things in a factory. How do you get someone to do those kinds of jobs? Besides creating economic pressures, you have to train them out of their passion.

Much of our education system was transplanted to our country from the Prussian system in the nineteenth century. The Prussians had lost to Napoleon. That wasn't good. They were either going to have to start speaking French or get their people in line. The Prussian people weren't fighting well; perhaps they were thinking too much about the pointlessness of fighting at all. The design of the Prussian system was in part to create obedience, but it was also designed to create less creativity, to mold the minds of young people into a perspective that aligned with authority by getting them to think less.

How do you get your citizenry to fall in line? You must destroy the individual passion and replace it with the obedience to the state. Without question, authoritative systems are more efficient, even in education. The Prussian system was well organized and measurable. Soon enough it was fashionable as well and was brought to this country, where it evolved into our current public education system. It is a system not of learning, but of destruction of the passion of the child. Its purpose is to mold the child to the will of the state and to produce workers. The Prussian system of the nineteenth century was designed to create a small percentage of students as the leaders; the bulk of the students were to serve the leaders, and the rest were uneducable and to be trained as workers. It was designed to sort the children for the good of the state. The state, of course, existed for the good of the elite, who design the schools.

Those who are able to sit in the front row of their class and get the right answers are going to rise to the top. For them the system works admirably, and they will continue to advocate for it as they live out their lives of privilege and power. For those who are the future workers, the poets, the non-standard learners, the hurt, the angry, the confused, something else has happened. They become co-opted into a cultural system that says, "You can't actually do what you love to do, but you can do something that will allow you to survive."

This works for the society. Does it work for people? Does it work for children? Does it work for all of us? Society is, after all, a social contract, an agreement among all of us.

And for that answer, you have to look inside your own life and see if your education cultivated your passion. Did your education free you, actualize you, and bring out your deepest qualities? Or did you survive your education and are you now just surviving your life? Did you learn to sit in the back rows, answer only when you knew that you had the right answer, take a job to pay the bills, and survive in your separate life, driving your financed car from your mortgaged condo? Perhaps you were an average student, molded into an average life. Or were you a blessed advanced learner, who perhaps cracked under the pressure along the way in school or in life? If you are none of these, are you still running as hard as you can to prove you belong in the front row?

Testing, Testing

One test of the correctness of educational procedure is the happiness of the child.

—Maria Montessori

Testing children's learning is an ill-conceived concept, yet so much a part of our notions of education that it is difficult to know where to begin in addressing the problem. And testing is a problem.

Testing is a problem because it has become a multi-hundred-million-dollar-a-year industry attempting to quantify the results of a public education system that is obviously not working, when the same money could be used to create and innovate. These dollar resources are being transferred from the local schools to the edu-corporations—from nonprofit, public institutions to private, for-profit companies.

Testing works in that it clearly divides students along socio-economic lines, it clearly divides students who know how to take tests from those who don't, and of course, it divides those who know the particular material being tested from those who don't. Why is this a problem? Don't tests quantify something about the amount learned? Doesn't this guide administrators and teachers in setting their agenda? Doesn't it help identify failing schools? No doubt it does all of these things, and despite the cultural corruption of favoring affluent kids and the waste of untold hours spent preparing for and taking these tests, they do work as designed.

The real problem with tests is that they don't do anything for children. Children experience fear, anxiety, boredom, and apathy in relation to tests. Tests don't have anything to do with children's needs.

Tests are tools of politicians, business interests, and education consultants. Tests won't help failing schools or failing children. If we feel moved to help, why don't we simply help? Tests won't do anything for children. They do something *to* children: turn them into statistics, give them labels, and stress them through the humiliation of imposed failure.

Tests have nothing to do with learning. They have nothing to do with teaching. They have nothing to do with relating to any particular child. They do not foster well-being, creativity, and joy.

No one seems to like tests—not parents, not teachers, and certainly not children. Yet the obsession with testing continues to intensify, as if more is better when none is best.

Tests seem to control the educational agendas of a growing number of public schools, reaching into the hearts and minds of more and more children. But tests have one fundamental weakness. They need us to care about them, to believe in them, to fear them.

What happens if we don't?

What if we say, "We won't take it any more?" We won't take the tests, or more accurately we won't agree to fund the testing process or put our children in the position of being forced to take the tests. Tests, like monsters under the bed, end when we cease to fear them, when we allow our children to ignore them, when we walk away from an idea whose time is long past.

Learning is not quantified by the authority of the test, but by the collaboration of those who share a learning environment and who can answer one simply question—a kind of test, if you will. What is the difference between a child and a statistic?

In educating the whole child, tests fail.

When the school environment we have created emphasizes tests, a student learns how to move through the testing process, which is what tests test, after all. Tests cannot measure how we integrate all that we know into all that we live. How could we test children for what they know? What they know has so many dimensions to it. Tests cannot test what they know, only what they don't know.

Tests don't teach children, people teach children.

During the time I was writing this book, I was invited to give a lecture to an undergraduate class on Education Theory at a large midwestern university. The topic was on learner-directed education. I understood that the students would be education majors, no doubt intensely interested in the subject of my talk, and I looked forward to seeing what young educators thought about what I had to say. But I learned just prior to the start of the class that, in fact, many of the students were taking the class to fulfill their humanities credit requirement and had no particular interest in the subject other than that it was considered an easy class to pass.

This was a fascinating situation in which to find myself. I was under the obligation to spend several hours talking to students who had no interest in what I had to say about interest-based learning. I wasn't even sure if I had anything to say to those who didn't care what I said. Should I stimulate interest by being entertaining? Should I concede the point and simply instruct, recognizing that I was in a lecture hall at a university where no one was ever asked about their interest? Should I confront the fact of the situation by walking out or demanding participation?

Like all moments, this moment as the talk began was rich with its own content and curiosity. The class itself, with all of its complex dynamics, hierarchical structures, studied disinterest, and feigned curiosity, was filled with students who were the product of years of conditioning to get through their schooling. They became the subject that interested me.

Despite the roles that we had taken on, I, as the author-
ity and teacher, and the students, with their chosen charac-
ters—the class clowns, the perky honor rollers, the sullen non-
participants, and the vacant dreamers—began to look at the
nature of learning.

This is how I began, that day: "This is going to be an
unusual class in this respect: the test is going to come first. Here
is the test. Can you look inside yourself, in this moment? What
are your drives? What are your fears? Can you see what you
are interested in? Can you see what your passion is? The test
is: who are you? That's the end of the test. You don't have to
take notes; there won't be another test. Does this interest you?"

Many of the class found that they, almost involuntarily,
became interested in what was discussed. My questions became
their questions as we began to explore together the quandary
we found ourselves in that day: the nature of interest and its
relationship to learning, the futility of stimulating interest by
being interesting, the dilemma of teaching those who were not
interested, the value of boredom as the spawning ground for
creativity, and how curious children become listless learners as
adults. It wasn't education theory that these students were
interested in, or any theory, really. Just like anybody, they were
interested in what was present in their lives, even if it hap-
pened to be in a lecture hall. Contact, candor, inquiry, and
relationship helped us to find each other, to touch each other
(at least for a few moments), and to rediscover the still vital
heart of learning.

Learning and Behavior

*School forcibly snatches away children from a world full of
the mystery of God's own handiwork, full of the suggestiveness
of personality. It is a mere method of discipline that refuses to
take into account the individual. It is a manufactory specially
designed for grinding out uniform results.*

—Rabindranath Tagore

The desire from within is the most direct motivation for a
child to learn. Does learning take place if it doesn't come
from within the child? We know that we can get a child to behave in particular ways through negative and positive coercion.
But can you force a child to learn, not just to behave?

When you put a rat in a maze and you reward that rat with
food for running down the maze, is the rat learning? Or is the rat
behaving? Is there a clear difference between the two?

Researchers may make no distinction. After all, the institutionalized education bureaucracy has such historic ties to behav-
iorist theories that it is no surprise that the differences between
coerced behavior and learning, between rat and child, have become blurred.

Operant conditioning and the promise of efficient models of
education that trained students with or without their interest or
cooperation through reward and punishment were a large part
of the brave new world that the baby boom generation entered.
The absurdity of this coldly rational and mechanistic view of the
human being was epitomized by the suggestion that even infants

could be adequately raised in boxes that would respond to and at the same time alter the child's needs.

But this sort of thinking influenced the notions of education. If a human being can be broken down into components of behavior and that behavior can be manipulated into useful patterns, then there is no distinction between learning and behavior. For the social engineer, this is a perfect system. The point of education, from this perspective, is to create productive citizenry from the raw material of mere children.

But the reality is that nobody likes being manipulated. Rats don't like it and neither do kids. Rats haven't figured out what to do about their dilemma other than to escape on occasion and reproduce wildly when given a chance. Children, precisely because they are extraordinary learners with tremendous creativity and spirit, have discovered all kinds of ways not to be conditioned: they rebel, they don't pay attention, they underachieve, they overachieve, they drop out, they withdraw, and so forth. Schools began identifying the various kinds of reactions and responded to each kind with a program, a therapy, a punishment, a reward, until the culture of the public school system has become an incomprehensible mess of conflicting intentions. It is no longer clear who is conditioning whom, only that something is fundamentally wrong. Worse, the education system appears more and more to be simply irrelevant.

This is all confusing. That bewilderment may be one of the healthiest qualities we could experience, because it leaves us less apt to settle for what we have created in our schools. But it also makes us a bit afraid.

We fear that a nonbehaving school, a nonbehaving population of children is a kind of anarchy. If children followed their own inclinations, what would give the world structure? Imagine that we are such children. How would our impulses be moderated? If I liked your sweater, why wouldn't I just take it? If I were bigger, wouldn't I just push you out of my way? We might fear that the world would become the world depicted in *Lord of the Flies*.

We don't need to fear that occurring, because it *has* occurred. We have the world that we fear. This is the world as it is—the world of the adults. Our fear is realized and we cannot run from it because we have children to raise.

How do we raise a whole child in the world we have today? Will the empowerment of the children in their own learning create chaos? Indeed it will if we give them only power and not responsibility and relationship. Empowering students to direct their own education includes the responsibility for the school community and everything that the school touches.

We are social animals; we are driven by our relationship to each other. Any group creates structure in its shared context. This social fabric is richer if everybody participates, but at the least, everyone must have the right to participate.

Relationship is simply more interesting than just me. This is what kids begin to learn at a young age. How do I have my relationship with you? I don't have it by taking your toy. You are going to walk away or fight with me. In either case you do not engage me in an enjoyable relationship. Relationship is what drives children and much of what they do is the exploration of its parameters.

The drive to relate can be stronger than the drive to power. In this regard, the presumption of anarchy doesn't seem to be accurate unless we exert a control over the children to break their relationship to each other. The anarchy we can expect in a small school where the participants exert self-rule is that of pure libertarianism, in which freedom is absolute so long as it does not infringe on the rights of another.

How will a self-directed, relationship-based learning environment structure itself? Will patterns simply emerge out of a chaotic movement of energies? Will it design itself politically, where those who have similar interests band together to be more effective in getting their needs met? That political structure is an integral part of the education because the students are intimately involved in its creation.

Why is it then that in virtually all but a handful of democratically run schools, the political environment is essentially totalitarian? It is top-down management, with an individual who runs the show, and some kind of fake practice democracy embedded in it. The student council decides the theme for the prom, but never anything more significant.

How do we expect the individual who comes through that system to emerge in a democratic society, when all that has been demonstrated is the fact that the powerful control? Won't these young people want to be powerful when they get their chance? And aren't we then creating generation after generation of individuals who want to overpower each other?

There is another possibility. If we don't create artificial power structures within a learning environment, doesn't the power really lie in relationship? I have to have enough relationship in order to get agreements. Power in a true democracy lies in deep relationship and the skills to communicate, to listen, and to forge creative solutions. Children who are allowed to work with each other in this way are quite capable of functioning democratically.

If we add a few adult staff into that learning environment, we create a problem. An inherent power structure appears. Adults are bigger. They know more. They are paid to show up at this place and their jobs are important to them. Now we have all these children running around in some form of relationship, and as a staff member, I'm not sure my job is secure. So I, the powerful adult, create a political structure in which I'm the administrator or I'm the teacher, but most importantly, I'm in control. We have a challenge when the adult enters this environment with the power that is invested in the nonchildren of the world. How do you equalize that?

In the highly structured educational environment where the adult is boss, at least you know they're boss, but in the progressive environment it can get more subtle, there can be a game of equality, except when it really matters. But if we are all equal, then we are equal especially when it matters. The word *equal* doesn't mean we're all the same; rather it is in reference to the power structure. A forty-year-old adult is not the same as a ten-year-old child. The adult holds a lot more information, a lot more experience, and presumably some wisdom as well. But in a democratic institution, a ten-year-old child is not less valuable than a forty-year-old adult, in terms of power.

The value of handing over not just power but responsibility in the relationships is that each person, young or old, is not just learning *in* that environment, but is learning *from* that environment. Further, each person brings valuable input *to* the situation. The whole child is now involved in the whole environment in everything from accessing information on the history of the French Revolution to helping to set up budgets for the school.

No one in this environment is granted more power than anyone else, and the group of children and adults can decide democratically what the rules are. This group can decide who should staff the school. Instead of just deciding on the theme for the prom, now you, as a child, have a right to participate in deciding whether I, as a staff member, actually connect with you in my capacity as a mentor. Of course, you, as a child, can also vote on the prom.

As a student, you may not be interested in the management of the school. You may be an eight-year-old who doesn't care about that and does not get involved in those meetings. You would be too absorbed by what you were interested in to get involved in something in which you weren't interested. But, you may be an eight-year-old who is decidedly concerned about the school environment. You then have the right to step forward and say, "This staff member shows up every day but he's not doing anything. Let's not hire him next year."

What does that do to the adult in that environment? Would it make the staff more interactive, more motivated, more responsive, more creative, more human? Let's imagine a society with no imbedded power structure. Would it be a more creative society? Would people be more energized to bring forth their innate creativity in such a world? Isn't this the world we want for our children?

Beyond Fear

Before I built a wall I'd ask to know
What I was walling in or walling out.
　　　　　　　　　　　　—Robert Frost

W ill we never take the risk of creating an egalitarian learning community because it is such a terrifying notion? It means, after all, that anybody in that community has a right to and the responsibility for relationship to all others. It can be quite comfortable to be in a power structure, regardless of where I am in it. I know there is somebody above me and someone below me. I know where I am located and I don't have to deal with the uncertainties of deep relationship. I don't have to handle the contact, the friction, and the depth that is demanded from whole living.

Beyond this fear of uncertainty is a vital question. Is there a way of structuring our world, our environment, our learning systems that is dynamic, fluidly moving with the whole? There is no answer to this question. There is not a fixed description of a way to do it; any system we create must be able to constantly recreate itself.

This is precisely why the systems of education that we have are failing. They are systems based only on information and thinking conceptually about that information. Thinking is a useful tool, but it always breaks the whole into parts and can never entirely synthesize the parts into the essential whole. Learning based on information and the manipulation of information fails simply because there is a great deal more to life than just that. Perhaps, more subtly, fragmented education of all kinds fails because it does not provide the integration, the synthesis of the pieces it teaches. Education limited to information and concept cannot teach the whole child and cannot foster what makes a useful life, a whole life, a happy life.

Children are not computers. The human being has the capacity to be conscious. We have the extraordinary ability to see the integrated whole and to live fully in and from that. Out of this understanding of a related life comes the flow of happiness, creativity, and love. This is the heart and the soul of learning.

Consciousness recognizes an interconnected whole that both you and I are part of. The human potential is the ability to be in a relationship-based system that is dynamic, moving, and changing. It could be the basis for all of our educational institutions. The endless creation that embodies the play of children is a simple example of this potential for self-organization, communication, and joy. Imagine this same quality brought into more sophisticated learning and life expression.

Integrated learning, whole learning, is incomprehensible to those infatuated with information; after all, they are the products of the learning systems they propagate. Acquisition of information was once the point of education, but that was before information exploded into the infinite permutations of the media, Internet, and computer. Now, integral intelligence—the awareness that utilizes but is not consumed by information—is what rules. This is the viewpoint that is in the information age, but not of it.

The dinosaurs that didn't adapt when the climate changed became fossil curiosities in museums. The educational climate has changed, is changing, and will change because true education *is* change. Change is so accelerated that the only learning that will be useful over a lifetime is learning that is adaptive and that also facilitates the student's capacity to change.

Whole learning has not been embodied in the education system, because the education system is in the past. This is not remedied by creating an education system that is futuristic, because that future is also going to change. To fully adapt, a learning system cannot be divided from all the other life systems that we are part of—the family, the society, the workplace—but is interwoven with those systems. A learning system must be open to the currents of spiritual, intellectual, physical, emotional, and artistic exploration circulating in society. For a learning system to be adaptive and for it to covey how to continuously learn, the system itself must be free of its own constraints, its own past, its own limitations. For a learning system to be whole, it too must be continuously learning, adapting, changing.

Anything less will fail in relation to a child who is dynamic, passionate, and fully alive. Children are amazingly tuned in to the limitation of whatever it is that we present to them. That is what they're about. They are limitation detectives. They go right to the limitation and they say, "What's on the other side of that?" It is a wonderful shared moment when we say, "Well, I don't know. Let's see what we can find out." That is the actuality of what we are all about, young or old. All of us are, in fact, in an inquiry about the nature of life. Any answer that stops the inquiry will fail. Any system of education that suggests that it knows creates a limitation, the boundary of its own knowledge. The boundary may contain a vast amount of knowledge, but it will not be enough for the whole child.

In the immense array of educational ideologies, none recognizes that no one knows how children learn. What if a core group of educators and parents recognized the fact that they don't know and that not knowing is a dynamic and energized state, the same state into which a child is born?

"I don't know" is the driving force of the child's learning. No discovery satisfies "I don't know." Everything the child learns only feeds the natural curiosity. The more the child discovers, the more the child doesn't know.

We don't need to create an ideology to capture that; we need to deconstruct the ideologies. What remains when we remove the limitations imposed by educational theory is the explosion of creativity. That creativity may take any number of forms, some so invisible to us that they wouldn't be recognized on a social level. There are individuals who live a very simple life with tremendous creativity. It may be the cashier at the grocery store or the bus driver. It may be the person who, like Albert Einstein, is a clerk who figures out how the universe works in his spare time. Einstein, Edison, and countless other creative geniuses also happened to be school dropouts. These remarkable creators came to greatness by breaking out of an education system that sought to contain them.

Thomas Merton once said, "Life is not a problem to be solved, but a mystery to be lived." Can we face the mysteriousness of life and can we give that mystery to the children, whose curiosity would drive them through the mystery into their own unknown? Can we actually create an environment in which we don't impose the conditioning that has been a disservice in our own lives— that has failed us, our parents before, and their parents before? Can we create a learning environment where that mystery is recognized, acknowledged, and made our constant companion?

The Happy Child in the Fragmented World

A man who has never gone to school may steal from a freight car, but if he has a university education, he may steal the whole railroad.

—*Theodore Roosevelt*

C an we imagine a happy child, educated by self-directed learning in an environment where wholeness is recognized and not overpowered? Imagine this passionate child growing up and emerging into the world, in all its chaos, just as it is.

What was learned in the whole-environment education that applies to the question of living as an adult? This young person has learned the skills of relationship, of communication, of creativity. He has learned how to direct his learning and his life. There is great confidence in these skills, because that confidence was not destroyed. This emerging adult was never systematically overpowered; the spirit was nurtured and allowed to explore. Most importantly, this whole adult was never taught the most heinous of lessons that most students learn day after dreary day: power is more important in human relationship than human relationship itself. Because this child (now an adult) was never indoctrinated into the cult of power, there is the possibility that she will actually be happy, that the heart will sing, that there will be a smile on her face in the morning because there is yet another day of curiosity, creativity, and relationship.

One parent—faced with the question of bringing her child into this kind of educational environment—said to me, "I am sure he would be tremendously happy here; I know he would. But what about college?" While it seemed a bit absurd that this parent would consider subjecting her child to an unhappy childhood so that he might get into a better college, this is what motivates many parents to rationalize their child's torment at the hands of traditional education. This same parent noted that her other son was just graduating from high school and could get into the college of his choice, but that he had absolutely no idea what he wanted to pursue. In twelve years of education, he had never had to formulate his own interests.

The self-directed learner knows a great deal about what interests him. But how does society look at this whole individual coming out of an alternative educational environment? The children who have come through public or private education and have had their initiative removed will, perhaps, seem somewhat similar to each other. The child who comes out of an unusual learning situation is likely to be unusual. Which has more value in any marketplace, the common or the scarce? The value of the unique is far greater.

Children in this kind of school will learn to identify their interests, organize resources around those interests, communicate to gather whatever resources are needed, set the rules of the environment with those around them, and face their own mind— their own boredom and their own interest. The child will learn to communicate, because no one is going to communicate on behalf of the child. It is not a passive environment; it is an environment that is self-creating.

How do such skills play out in the world at large? Adults with these skills are the leaders, the entrepreneurs, the artists, the cultural creatives. These skills equip a young person for success and, more importantly, allow that success to be defined not by the society, but by the inner spirit of the individual. This is the potential of a happy child.

Parents often fear that such an unusual child won't get into college and will not be viable economically. But colleges are hungry for the unusual student. Their admissions committees are bored and exhausted by the endless stream of standardized applicants. Long-standing democratic schools report an extremely high rate of acceptance in colleges by those graduates who chose to go on with their formal education.

The parent's fear is really an economic fear. It's a fear of the nonsurvival of the child, which, in a way, is the parent's neurotic obligation to the child. It is the parent's job to worry. But that fear is also in response to the myth that we will survive only through playing the game of institutionalized education.

It is not hard to provide kids with a safe place to gather and learn, tools, resources, mentors, and guides. It is not hard to recognize that kids are born with the instinct to learn and to create. Kids don't need our help to learn how to learn; they know what interests them. This is where their attention and energy go; magically, learning takes place. Interest creates learning, and they want to learn about what makes them happy.

Happy kids? This could be a problem. Happy kids could mean happy adults and then what would the world come to? Wouldn't kids left to their own direction just watch television all day? Who would learn anything? Don't we need them to learn so they can eventually go to work and watch a computer screen all day? We say we are afraid that self-directed children won't learn, but we can be sure that they will learn to be self-directed. Perhaps a self-directed child is what we are really afraid of.

Let's look at this question from a very nonspiritual, nonprogressive vantage point. Let's look at it from a purely capitalistic standpoint. If we are trying to fit children into the workplace, what will that workplace be like in fifteen or twenty years when they are done with school? Will the computer or the human be doing the algebra? Which will remember more history? Which will spell better? Which would you acquire for your company to handle computation: a human at $35,000 per year plus benefits, vacation, and sick days, or a computer at $2,000 plus electricity and occasional upgrades?

Corporations can order more computers to handle information and computation, but they cannot find enough decision makers, creative troubleshooters, communicators, and relationship-based managers. This is simply because those qualities are not fostered in our education system; rather, they are methodically stripped from students year after year.

Corporate management is clogged with people who don't know how to make decisions or who are simply afraid to. They never had to decide much because they went through an education system that decided everything for them. All they had to do was pass the tests.

The Japanese government recently began revising its education system to reduce the hours of school, to reduce the amount of information taught by one-third, and to turn away from rote memorization. Furthermore, it is introducing short periods of integral study each day in which students are asked to exercise their creative thinking and independently pursue their interests in order to nurture a zest for living. Why would a country that ranks at the top of the entire world in math and science knowledge begin tinkering with its renowned education system? The president of IBM's Asia Pacific Operations, quoted, not in the *Harvard Educational Review,* but in *The Wall Street Journal,* says, "What we need are the kind of people who can create new things, to rise to new challenges, and to think of how to produce results on their own. We no longer need people who simply get good grades." Japan has enough workers; it has an acute shortage of the creative thinkers, entrepreneurs, and just plain individuals now required by the post-industrial economy.

It is not only that business needs creative problem solvers rather than people conditioned to obey, to repeat, to not think, and to sit still like components of some past-tense industry. It is clear that the individual's life is better served through this creative, self-confident, and relationship-based learning. The creative individual is better for the whole of society as well.

Perhaps we will realize, after a long and troubled infatuation with business, that we do not live for business, but that business lives for us, all of us. But more to the point of our lives, it is the need for a fundamental response to our world of violence, cultural fragmentation, environmental degradation, and the ignorance of miseducation and misunderstanding. This radical change is already active and alive in each child. Is it possible for us to allow each child to be whole, to be happy, and to face the challenge of the world as it is with the fullness of the human potential?

The Failure of Education

Education is an admirable thing, but it is well to remember
from time to time that nothing worth knowing can be taught.
— Oscar Wilde

E ducation makes one fundamental mistake. It exists. Education supposes that it has something to impart, and it is from this flawed perspective that all of its problems flow. Holistic learning is not transactional; it is interactional. Far from having something to teach, education has something to learn: it is not necessary; it just needs to get out of the way.

Education as it has come to be practiced in our society is the destruction of the child. Born into curiosity and driven by the innate need to learn, children are herded into prisonlike institutions, forced through threats to unnaturally sit in hard chairs and memorize the most preposterous bits of disconnected information. They are coerced through punishment and reward to perform on tests, behave according to arbitrary rules, and not communicate with each other. Their teachers are themselves victimized, forced to play a particular character, to behave and react in particular ways, and to present prepackaged information in which the teacher has no real interest. This truly bizarre situation is not only failing to produce creative individuals; it is sinking into the abyss of its own violence.

Today's schools have too little to do with learning and too much to do with control, indoctrination, and destruction of the human spirit. Whether these schools are the most run-down of public schools or the endowed private schools, if they take the freedom out of learning they serve to destroy the natural curiosity of the child and replace it with mechanical behavior and poverty of spirit.

Democratic Learning

Individual and Society

It is well to remember that the entire universe, with one trifling exception, is composed of others.
                                                              —*John Andrew Holmes*

A learning community where the participants are free to decide the conditions of their education sets the stage for an essential understanding. The free learner, understanding the related nature of the school community in which he is fully empowered, can easily see the purpose of participation in decision making and the obvious consequences in failing to abide by the rules that are mutually agreed upon.

The flow of information and ideas in such a place is unhampered, and the evidence is present in existing schools that embody elements of self-direction; participants create an ever-evolving flow of projects, classes, businesses, relationships, debates, and individual explorations. Schools like the Sudbury Valley School, Summerhill, and the Albany Free School, among others, are long standing, highly visible, and remarkably successful examples of democratic learning communities. By allowing this milieu of creative expression, these schools have tapped into a seemingly endless source of educational innovation and creativity—the students themselves.

Tremendous time, money, and energy is expended in educational institutions on controlling the student population, which in turn expends its energy rebelling both passively and aggressively. In a democratic-learning community, the individual is unhampered other than by community considerations, and the community is unburdened of the need to restrict and control. There is the possibility of a synergistic intelligence occurring in which the student, without losing any of the unique expression of individuation, may also understand the fundamental reality of interrelatedness.

We do not need to mold children to be part of society, nor do we want to encourage an anarchistic expression of self-interest. What is possible is the understanding of the nested reality, the interconnected reality of the individual and the all. This is the human potential, not as taught by a seminar or self-help book, but as the emerging expression of the children themselves. This is holistic learning, in which the child is left alone to learn, to interact, to err, to correct, to relate, to love.

Compulsory Education

I hated school so intensely. It interfered with my freedom. I avoided the discipline by an elaborate technique of being absent-minded during classes.
    — Sigrid Undset (1928 Nobel Prize in Literature)

When we consider the notion of learner-directed education, we cannot avoid the question of how the learning community distributes power, decision making, and control of resources.

We are used to systems that pass the power immediately to adults with the rationale that children are not responsible enough to handle such decisions. Children, keying on the cues from the adults, often fulfill those expectations by not being responsible. This circular argument has gone on for as long as public education has existed. Ironically, this is the same education system that brought children in, by force, from the farms and factories where they labored, often under horrendous conditions, but in full responsibility. It would appear that children have the capacity for freedom and responsibility, but they have been turned into dependents long past the age where it is necessary. Childhood, if we include an endless adolescence, has been extended to decades.

The first attack on the child's freedom to learn in our country came in Massachusetts in 1852 with the first forced public schooling. The notion that the state has the authority to require a child to go to school and that it is best for a country to have an educated population would appear at first glance to be a well-considered social policy. But at the heart of mandatory education is the position of the state as superior to parents in directing the upbringing of their children and, for that matter, the child's freedom to direct his or her own life.

Americans, who created their country out of a refusal to have their individual rights made inferior to those of the state and who resist government control of everything from guns to pornography, have accepted the right of the state to educate their children. Compulsory education, besides dramatically infringing on the individual's rights, has a second, more subtle side effect: it forces schools to warehouse students who have no interest in being in school. While the state can require parents to deliver their children to a school, every child knows that no one—parent, principal, police, or politician—can deliver their heart and soul, their attention and intention, their engagement in learning. A large segment of every school population is made up of educational conscientious objectors, those who will not cooperate with the compulsory draft of thought control. These students know that nobody ever asked them what they wanted for their life, or if the school environment had anything to offer them, or if they had vital agendas that were being obstructed by the imposition of forced schooling. They are angry, and what they end up learning in school is how to subvert the system, get by, pass through, or drop out.

A student who doesn't want to be in school doesn't belong there—first, because she has the innate right of personhood that an egalitarian society bestows on each of us, and second, because it is pointless to warehouse a disinterested student in the name of education. Where do they belong? Let us ask them where they would like to be. Perhaps some would choose to work, or apprentice, or learn independently, or do nothing at all while they figure out what they really love. If schools let them explore these options, or, dare we suggest, actually supported them in these pursuits, the distaste for school would disappear. What adults have come to believe is that these students who don't want to be in school will be idle schemers, ne'er-do-wells, and criminals. Of course, this is often what angry students forced into school become anyway. And while it is likely that criminals are not interested in going to school, it is not the disinclination for school that creates the criminality. It is the complex, destructive surroundings and broken relationships that many young people find themselves enmeshed in at their homes and in their communities.

Teachers don't want to teach those who don't want to learn. Learners don't want to learn from teachers with whom they don't have any relationship or about subjects in which they have no interest. School boards, administrators, politicians, and police are burdened by the cost and difficulty of managing sullen, defiant, or downright violent students. Escalating violence, once easily dismissed as an inner-city issue, is a potential in every school. Are the incidents of mass violence just the work of crazies—pathetic psychotic anomalies—or are they, in part, symptoms of a system that no longer works and cannot work? More security cameras and guards, police patrols, and students informing on each other to authorities will not stop the violence. The context for violence begins to take shape when freedom is taken away and responsibility is not allowed.

Perhaps these young people would have a different relationship if they were stakeholders in their own learning environment, involved in the creation, management, and ultimately the success or failure of their own schools. You cannot give a person the responsibility to operate an institution at the same time as you make him a prisoner. You cannot remove all responsibility for a person's environment and expect him to want to be there. But if you give anyone freedom and responsibility, an alchemy takes the energy of anger and rebellion and molds it into engagement and creativity.

A society that is free cannot educate its children in anything less than freedom. Is it unclear why our society, educated by force now for more than a century, accepts more and more limitations on its own freedom and expression?

Forced Curriculum and the Creatures of the State

*If we were all alike, it might be convenient for the bureaucrat
and the statistician, but it would be very dull, and would lead
to a very unprogressive society.*

—*Bertrand Russell*

What should a student learn in school? This seems like an obvious question to ask when we are considering a democratic society. Who decides what our children will learn? Will it be university educators, foundations, textbook publishers, politicians, local school boards, or teachers? All of these brokers of curricula are continuously wrestling for control and influence. Creationism or evolution? Whole word reading or phonics? Is it core knowledge accountability or is it teaching to the test? The world of educational theory is constantly split, faction against faction, with billions of dollars at stake and, almost as an afterthought, the lives of our children as well.

Subtler than the infighting of educational theologians over dollars and power is the damage done by the narrowing of knowledge to the limited range that *any* expert sees as important. This movement to a standardized set of factoids in the guise of education is potentially short-circuiting the diversity of viewpoint and energy of dialogue that make a democracy vital. If the population of any society learns through an institutionalized and nationalized curriculum, won't that society become stagnant through the continuous imprint of its own mediocrity? Don't standards begin to exist for their own continuation, with their own bureaucrats, and enforced by their own power structures? The free flow of ideas, information, and considerations comes to a halt because only certified information is taught and tested. Only those tested and passed move into positions of power, and only those in positions of power determine the certification of information taught.

A totalitarian control of what is taught and learned is the beginning of the end of democratic structures. Democracy requires egalitarian treatment of learning, freedom of information, and openness to the expression of all forms of education.

The First Amendment to the United States Constitution prohibits laws that restrict the freedom of speech. Those who framed the structures of a democratic society saw the free flow of information as an important counterforce against the tyranny of centralized power. It is not difficult to see the connection between the control of how an individual is educated and the resultant restriction on the capacity and range of expression. The United States Supreme Court has occupied itself over and over again with challenges to this most basic of rights. But it was not until 1925 that the Supreme Court in the United States struck down an Oregon state statute that required children to attend public schools exclusively *(Pierce v. Society of Sisters of Holy Names)*. The court declared it beyond the power of any state to "standardize its children" by stopping parents from finding alternatives to public schools. It wrote that a child is not "the mere creature of the state," and that the state could not unreasonably interfere with "the liberty of parents and guardians to direct the upbringing and education of children under their control."

Over subsequent decades, the Supreme Court prohibited unreasonable regulation of private and religious schools. Finally, in 1992 *(Martin),* the Court protected home schooling. There has been slow but consistent recognition that the consolidation of education into a nationalized structure undermines democracy. There is a direct connection between preserving individual freedom of intellect, of belief, and of education and the resultant cultural diversity that makes up a healthy, egalitarian society.

Can a nation enjoy freedom of speech if it does not maintain freedom of education, which, after all, influences that speech? While the price we pay for freedom of speech is often the presence of forms of expression we neither agree with nor enjoy, the overriding good of the society and the quality of life for each individual is enhanced by that general freedom. Is education any different in substance? If there is to be no freedom of expression in learning, then how shall we decide who or what controls the minds of students?

Debate and Decision Making
in Learning

*When ideas go unexamined and unchallenged for a long
enough time, certain things happen. They become mythologi-
cal, and they become very, very powerful. They create
conformity. They intimidate.*

— *E. L. Doctorow*

The political history of education and the ensuing policy debate may seem tedious and without obvious end, but underlying the politics is an interesting question: can true learning
take place where students are forced, not just in attendance, but
in the restriction of movement, mind, and spirit that takes place
in a school?

Can a child who has the entire context of his life and his school
environment dictated to him understand anything other than the
nuances of the environmental dictates (behavior) and the absorption of information (memorization)? We could say that behaving
and memorizing are a type of learning, but certainly not the holistic learning that takes into account problem solving and complex decision making, and includes relationship to the entire
environment. Rote learning produces skills, but they are skills of
parroting and, as we know, parrots need a trainer to perform.

Is this what we want for our children, that they be molded
through behavior modification and informed through indoctrination? This is what has become of the public schools and
many of the private schools as well. Perhaps this is why the

problem-solving capacity of students has fallen over the past decades, while their IQ test scores have continued to rise.

A child does not just need the full range of freedom to explore, experiment, and truly learn. Without freedom, there is no chance to learn responsibility. Mostly we teach what we call responsibility by solving problems for the students in a school, embodying those solutions in rules of conduct, and enforcing those rules. Those who rebel, who demand freedom and take responsibility for that demand by acting outside of the controlling rules, are punished or become outcasts. Those who comply are considered responsible citizens by those who control the school. But this is not responsibility; again, it is merely behavior.

Responsibility requires freedom. Each individual needs to have the space to fail in that responsibility, to suffer the consequences of the failure, and to be redeemed by accepting those consequences. This exploration of the interplay of personal desire and the social contract in the society of a school is the pathway to understanding a relationship-based life. Unconscious behavior won't work in freedom; it breaks down, and the shadow side emerges. It is only with each person's examination of this essential question, in freedom, that the individual integrates the drives of the psyche with the connection to others.

Schools that control take away not only the student's freedom, but also their responsibility. Learning can take place despite such a place, and it is remarkable that it does. This is a tribute to the resiliency of the learning mind and the human spirit.

Freedom and Responsibility: You Can't Have One without the Other

My teachers saw me at once backward and precocious, reading books beyond my years and yet at the bottom of the Form. They were offended. They had large resources of compulsion at their disposal, but I was stubborn. Where my reason, imagination or interest were not engaged, I would not or I could not learn.
—Winston Churchill

Part of learning is understanding real discipline; not the false discipline resulting from external threat, but the natural integration of our inner drives. We often try to teach kids discipline by forcing them to do something that they don't want to do, rather than by asking them to see the consequences of their actions and to take responsibility for their words, deeds, and the reactions of those around them. Discipline is not just being able to do the thing that we don't want to do, but also being able to do the hard thing that we *do* want to do.

There are things that we don't enjoy, yet we will also quite naturally discipline ourselves to do, because we understand that the activity that we don't like allows us to do something that we do like. If I want to be a long distance runner, I don't want to do that first four or five weeks of training, because it's difficult and painful, but I understand that I have to break through that to enjoy the sport. We all have examples in our lives where we put ourselves through experiences we didn't like because we knew that it was related to some goal.

In a democratically run learning community there are rules that everyone agrees upon. That is a discipline that's exerted from a community to a person who may not feel like following the rules. Because the structure is democratically generated, each member of the school community has the opportunity to take part in creating it. Rebelling in this context takes on a different meaning and brings a different kind of response. Breaking a rule is a violation of my community and my peer group, and this community will respond in enacting the consequent punishment.

This kind of relationship-based discipline is fundamentally different from a school administrator who is empowered to make the rules. In the traditional power structure, all that can happen is the student either gives up his autonomy or rebels. There is no space for engagement and dialog.

In a democratic environment, if students spend three hours with compatriots at the school debating whether a rule is a good idea or not, whether it has social utility or not, and whether there are any examples of schools run with or without this particular rule, in the end everyone involved understands the nature of this particular agreement. Then, when that rule is voted on and passed, even if the majority was slight, even if you disagree with it, every person understands that something happened that is about them. This is the real power of non-hierarchical structures, and this power, of course, is available to anyone who participates.

Learning and Belief: The Strange
Case of the Missing Reality

Culture and Perspective

A great many people think they are thinking when they are
merely rearranging their prejudices.

— *William James*

Recently, I walked through a store with one of my young children. I was distracted for a few moments by my purchase and my son became captivated by a television monitor in the corner broadcasting smarmy offers for products of one kind or another. He joined me after a few minutes and began repeating the jargon of the piped-in come-on, intrigued by the promise that he could join in the wonderful world that was promised by the toy, the movie, or the drink simply by buying something. My son had learned something. I had learned something too. No one had asked me if it was all right to sell my son something. And no one will in the future. My son is a market share, however small, and marketers will find him wherever he goes.

The culture's perspective and my son's perspective are in constant interaction, and much of that interaction will have to do with a relationship to materialism. The market will promise happiness, but it can deliver only goods and services. What my son is learning from his culture is that goods and services are the same as happiness. What is important to me is that he have the opportunity to find out, for himself, whether this is true. His understanding will make up his life.

It is impossible to address the question of educating our children without taking on the difficult task of understanding the culture in which the child learns. In the contemporary western culture, we are subject to powerful media forces that condition our perspectives in complex ways. We can hardly move about in society without ingesting marketing of one product or another. More insidious is the omnipresence of brands, representing entire lifestyles and evoking feelings of freedom, happiness, and accomplishment through the choice of the proper can of soft drink or designer jeans.

This crass, materialistic society is teaching us constantly. Marketing is education, but what is taught is consumption, not consideration. Reflection on the nature of the market forces is not desirable from a marketing standpoint. This is why marketing always tries to co-opt the consumer by creating fads, tendencies, and urges just below the threshold of considered action. Marketing speaks in hyperbolic or subliminal language, seldom in accurate or factual terms. It is fundamentally dangerous to our children to be unaware of the impact of these forces on their minds.

Children who have been given responsibility and the freedom to exercise it develop critical thinking as an obvious by-product of their circumstance. They have the chance to explore what brings them satisfaction and what does not. The child whose discrimination and will has been broken down by years of coercive education is a perfect candidate to be a pliant consumer of whatever is being sold. Of course, what is sold must be produced, and the pliant consumer is also a docile worker.

To educate our children in a new way, we must understand our culture—the social contracts and paradigms that make up our collective perspective. The forces of mass marketing and consumerism come out of deeply entrenched patterns in our society and its history. They reflect the very structures of mind and biology that make up the individual. If we can understand something about our individual and collective reality, we can hope to create a learning environment that is something more than just an indoctrination into our conflicted world.

We have all learned the maxim that failure to learn from history will force us to repeat its patterns. This seems simple enough. But we must also understand the perspective from which we learn this history. If we fail to see the perspective that defines that history, we can create only more of that same perspective. We will impose a concept of nationality, race, religion or any number of other imbedded interpretations over the actuality of what has occurred.

The hidden vantage point—our blind spot, the cultural ego and identification—is a source of our irresolvable world problems, and its unraveling is the beginning of the solution. We teach this hidden perspective in our schools, but we seldom teach about it. We don't consider our cultural perspective to be just one of many perspectives.

Our culture often is stranger than fiction—it sometimes appears to *be* fiction. The merger of information, advertising, and entertainment in a media-saturated environment leaves us wondering what reality is, or worse, *if* it is. No wonder we turn to belief systems to give ourselves certainty. If we embrace certainty, it is only because we stand, in fact, in uncertainty, and that is uncomfortable. But the certainty of belief, when taught as fact, is indoctrination, not education.

Whole learning requires the understanding of the nature of belief itself. This learning includes the deep questioning of all perspectives. The whole learner meets every assumption with a question.

It is not necessary to mechanically repeat the past by creating the future in its image. We do not need to educate our children into a form of life destined to repeat the failures of history by repeating its hidden cultural perspectives. We do not need to condition our children to understand the world in all its dimensions exactly as the dominant history suggests they should.

We can invite our children to join with us in discovering a new way of living, a way that melds the fresh perspective of childhood with the knowledge of the adult. This is a new kind of wisdom that finds as its basic perspective the happiness of each of us and all of us. In this we neither lead the child nor are lead by the child, but are co-creators, each lending our strengths, respectful of the other's autonomy and grounded in deep connectedness. It is possible that together we can discover what is more than the sum of the parts: the relatedness that we all feel deep in our being, and the expression in all the forms of our world that embodies a happy life for all. There is no greater gift to our children and no higher aspiration in the education that we give them. If they are allowed to, they will receive this gift and pass it on to their children with great happiness.

Thought as Technology

One of the main legitimate functions of thought has always been to help provide security, guaranteeing shelter and food, for instance. However, this function went wrong when the principle source of insecurity came to be the operation of thought itself.

—David Bohm

What are we teaching our children? This is not just a question of what subject to teach, or even what values to teach, but the need to understand the essence of the reality that we are conveying. In education, we have actively chosen the development of thinking, conceptualization, and abstraction as the most valued elements of learning. The seduction of information and intellect is so strong that we are only beginning to remember that there are qualities in life worth learning that have nothing to do with information at all. Thinking skills are not the only area worth teaching to our children, and yet this is the area that is immensely overdeveloped in our school systems. The capacity for linear thinking is easily measured, tested, and quantified as a direct result of our educational dollars.

But why are we so enamored with this one faculty of the human being that we have built our entire culture around it? Thought, after all, is only one way to understand the world, and only relatively recently has it come into vogue as the best way to do so. Yet the conceptual mind, more than any other human capacity, characterizes the structure of our society.

In the seventeenth century, Descartes wrestled for a long time with his difficulty in believing in thought as an accurate representation of the world. He felt that thought could be deluded, that it could be illusory; but, if so, then what was there to hang onto? This was pretty scary, so he capitulated. Thought, he decided, was probably the best thing we had to identify us and everything else. If not thought, then what? This was a great question, and since existentialism hadn't been invented yet, it was really a showstopper. If not thought, then there really isn't anything you can think about, and....poof...there goes reality.

Descartes thought about this a great deal and decided he would rather exist than not. He said, "I think, therefore I am."

And we believed him.

So, what we began to live was: "I believe, therefore I am." We built a world based on our belief in thought and on the notion that "I am." We built a marvelous society based on thinking and the separation of the individual thinker of those thoughts.

Now we cannot find our way out of the maze, but we cannot completely believe in the maze either. The maze of thought is interconnected, but it connects us in separation, like suburban tract home developments where we live in a community, but we don't know our neighbors.

Evolutionary biologists suggest that thinking developed as a skill to identify food resources and strategies to acquire them. Memory developed as a means to remember where we left our food supplies and how to get back to them. Today, thought continues to design our life so that we survive. It is not so concerned that we are happy; this is not the job of thinking. Thought knows a lot about the theory of happiness, but not much about its actuality. If we are concerned that our children are happy, then they must develop their thinking capacity so they will survive, and develop a great deal more than their thinking so they can live a fulfilled life.

We live in proximity to each other in thought, but we cannot fully connect to each other in that area; too much ideology is in the way, and too much survival instinct. Something else besides our ideas connects us to each other: a quality of heart and feeling, the perception of commonality that has little to do with our education, but something to do with the qualities of relationships we have experienced with our teachers and fellow students, with our family and friends.

Thought is a great tool. It has allowed us to produce the world of technological wonder that we see all around us. Thought allows us to model, predict, and manipulate the world. We can hold the world in our perceptual field or in the field of our imagination, representing it in conceptual form. We can use that model to extrapolate the possibilities for the future. Using thought, we can attempt to change that future in order to minimize any danger to ourselves. We can represent all of this in language.

This mental capacity is extraordinary. We can think, model, predict, and manipulate, and, as a result, we will survive. Except it is not "we" that will survive, it is "me" that will survive. This wonderful technology has a small programming bug, like an unstoppable, replicating computer virus. The glitch is "me." The program runs really well, but what survives when all of the modeling, predicting, and manipulating dust settles is not necessarily the common good.

This fragmented sense of self, growing out of unintegrated thought, uninformed by all the other dimensions of life, does not have the capacity to think holistically, but only individualistically.

Our culture is built on these fragments and educates each generation from this perspective. The overemphasis on the education of thinking without regard for its integration into the whole of life is simply amplifying this tragic evolutionary wrong turn. The rugged individual will go the way of the really rugged dinosaurs if that sense of self is not mitigated by a sense of space, community, and relationship. The sense of individuality is important, vital, and irreplaceable, and needs to be fostered. But that individual, as a fact of life, is in relationship to all that is in life; this realization brings wisdom, compassion, and sustainability to the separate self. The freedom of the individual need not be impeded by anything other than the deep sense of responsibility and connection that is the natural expression of the human being.

In our infatuation with the thinker—a single dimension of the spectrum of the human experience—we have created a culture of selfishness that takes pride in its separation. We educate our children to compete, testing for their accomplishments and rewarding those who excel by surviving and surmounting. We reward individualism without suggesting its interrelatedness with the whole of life.

We have forgotten the limitations of the function of thought and created a psychological identification with it. Thought is a technological gizmo, and we are so much more. The individual who is only an individual is living at far less than the full capacity of the human being. Our human potential is to be uniquely, even eccentrically individual *and* in full relationship to the whole of life. But we never learned that at school. There are no tests designed to measure that. The integrated human being does not stand above all others; he stands with all others.

What if Descartes, facing the question of self, had realized the integral self rather than the separate self? What if he had declared, "I love, therefore I am"? What if we had believed this and built our society around the connection to each other, a society where giving, helping, and healing were valued and the function of thought was to facilitate a compassionate life? In such a society, what would a school be like and what would it teach?

Dare we question our identification with our own knowledge? Can we find a perspective on thought that returns it to its function and recognizes its limitations? Can we find a perspective that encompasses the thinker of thought in the fact of our interconnectedness? Can we find a kind of intelligence that recognizes thought as a tool, but the whole of life as the context?

What does education become if it is broader than the concepts that it teaches, broad enough to teach the whole child?

Nothing: What You've Been Looking For

"Sometimes you can observe a lot by watching."
—*Yogi Berra*

When we teach children that information is the most important element in an education, we are subtly selling them on a value system that is imbedded in our culture. Information has decreasing utility. Over time, much of what we learn becomes dated or irrelevant. Our world has too much information and not enough context. What serves our children is not simply endless streams of information, but the intelligence to organize and utilize it. It is the relationship to information, not information itself, that defines intelligence.

The information overload in our schools is a reflection of a culture that is obsessed with information and commerce, or information as commerce. Stock market quotes run across our television screens as we watch the news; in-between are commercials for products we are just learning we need. We scan the newspaper before we drive to work, listening to the news while we drive.

What is it we are looking for? We are accumulating information at an ever-increasing rate, but what is the point of it all? In the ongoing frenzy of discovering and recording more and more information, we have lost the context, the motivation behind the action.

This is the brave new world of information saturation, where data is bought and sold, where the individual is reduced to a statistical buying pattern. The message is consumption, and the medium is everything from the names of our sports stadiums to the pockets of the shirts we wear. There is nothing that isn't a commodity if it is packaged and sold. There is even a market for nothing, if you know how to sell.

A short time ago in New Zealand, a young graphic designer was thinking about advertising and all its strangeness, its coercive ability to sell the most completely bizarre things to people who usually don't need them. He created a brilliant social experiment.

The designer considered what the most nonexistent product would be and decided to market ... Nothing™. With billboards all over Auckland touting, "Nothing™—What you've been waiting for," and carrying the obligatory image of a beautiful woman looking off into the distance, the phones began to ring with callers who were ready to buy what they already presumably had plenty of.

The Nothing™ campaign showed something about the power of money to sell, the power of image to communicate a need that consumers did not even realize they had. Perhaps, most importantly, it demonstrated that even nothing could become something in the world of information.

If nothing can become something, then how do we know that everything isn't nothing? What if everything is simply packaged nothing that has been cleverly inserted into our minds as not just important, but essential? What if everything is nothing bundled up with attractive images and sold to us as ... what we've been looking for?

That is the promise of information. It tells us that what we are looking for is more, better, total information. This is the core of our contemporary education. If we can pack in enough information, we will have everything.

What if everything is not really what we've been looking for? What if the marketing of information has convinced us to accumulate more of everything, more of nothing, more of anything? What if none of that is what we are looking for? Yet we educate our children as if the endless stream of information is what they should be looking for.

The culture of endless marketing churns on, relentlessly.

Every place we look we see the corporate logo. More™. More™ Stadium. Brought to you by More™ (so you will buy more). Designed by More™. Sponsored by More™. And there's more.

Billboards that show a beautiful woman or a muscled young man with the slogan, "More™ ... What you've been looking for." Or simply: "Buy More™."

And when we look at these messages, what do we experience? Do we feel that somehow we are missing something if we don't have more? Or do we have the unsettling feeling that the message, the medium, the information-as-its-delivery is unrelated to what we are in fact looking for?

Do we actually feel that if small is beautiful, then less is joyous? Do we look at the information streaming towards us from all directions, and like futurist aikido masters, let the information flow on by into the nether world of Nothing™?

What happens to the message when the medium is awareness? What if our counter-marketing campaign is "Awareness™ ... What we're looking from?"

Awareness doesn't need more information. It needs only enough information. This intelligence, the quality that mediates information into wisdom, is seldom referenced in school. If we do not include awareness in what we convey to our children, then aren't we teaching them to be unconscious and to be consumers of an endless stream of pointless information and products?

The young child inhabits a vast array of kinds of intelligence held in the body/mind. Their need for information is intense, but it is mediated by the other capacities of their system—their feelings, sensations, and body appetites for movement and play. We can channel all of their life energy into the absorption of information, but without the intelligence of the whole child, we will produce adults who have a great deal of fragmented data, but have integrated nothing.

The New Docudrama Reality:
The Merger of Fact and Fiction

All my life I wanted to be somebody. I can see now I should
have been more specific.

— *Steven Wright*

J ust the facts. Traditional education suggests that it teaches
the facts. Perhaps in a simpler time, there were clear facts.
Today, we have a complex world in which the way we construct and understand what is real is undergoing fundamental
change. Computer generated virtual worlds, televised imagi-
nary worlds, and the incredible events of the actual world re-
ported to us through incessant media all compete for their place
in our reality. How will we teach our children to navigate in a
universe in flux? What is the intelligence that sorts through the
mass of the media and finds the qualities worth embodying?

In the wilds of Maryland, a friendly camping trip starts in-
nocently enough before ending in tragedy, all captured on tape
by a shaky, hand-held video camera. Except it is not a home video.
It is a documentary. Except it is not a real documentary. It is a
fictional movie made in documentary style. It is about an encounter with a witch after all. That should be a clue that this is
fiction, not fact. *The Blair Witch Project* is just a story, just a breakthrough movie.

In another city, the door is being kicked in at the scene of a
domestic dispute turned violent. As the cops rush in to subdue

the drunken man and make the arrest, we hear a voice-over explaining what is happening; we remember that we are watching television. This is just a made-for-television docudrama. Well, we're partly right. It is made for television. It is dramatic. But what we are watching is an actual police action, camera crews filming the whole thing as it happens, commentary provided by the cop who is kicking in the door; the other actors are just pathetic people who happen to be breaking the law on camera. This is fact, not fiction.

Cops is a breakthrough reality television show.

On television, on any given day, we can watch talk shows with guests whose real lives are stranger then any fiction. Hosts who are actors pretend to care about their guests and the viewers at home. The television personality performs in front of an audience, coached by the show director to act excited about the show, clap when the applause sign comes on, and otherwise be visually animated when the camera is on them. Flashing on the screen after the commercial break are invitations to call the show's toll free number if your life is particularly deviant and you'd like to share your aberrations with millions of voyeurs. Some guests get on the show by faking it—that is, making up something weird about their life. While some effort is made to weed them out, mostly they are exposed on the show itself, which makes them appear that much stranger and makes the ratings that much higher. As viewers, we pretend that we are not really interested in this carnie sideshow, that we just happened on the program and are interested from a sociological vantage. But, of course, we keep watching, because these real people are living out our darkest fantasies, our most frightening nightmares, and just occasionally, our fondest dreams. We are not sure if these programs are really fact or fiction; the borders are getting a little gray. This is fact *and* fiction.

Now, go on the Internet and you'll find some fascinating reality being produced. In one house occupied by nine coeds, cameras mounted throughout the home broadcast everything going on in the house, twenty-four hours a day. You can watch these young ladies sleep, eat, bathe, dress, and undress; the imagination runs wild. It is supposed to. Because you can watch only for a monthly fee billed directly to your credit card. It is a business, as it turns out. But it is all real. Sort of. The women are paid to live in the house. The website is run by a brilliant pornographer. And it is all a fact, created from the imagination and entrepreneurial vision of a businessman. This is fictional fact.

Over on MTV you can find *Real World*. It's actually another television show. The producers have put together a household of people with no script to follow, let them live their lives, tracked them with cameras, and created a hugely popular soap opera that is actually happening. There have been little problems along the way, like the young cast member who almost died from alcohol poisoning as she drank and drank while the cameras watched and watched. That's why MTV calls it *Real World*; like that thing in the Bible, are we our brother's keeper when there is a show to produce? *Real World* is factual fiction.

If *Real World* is factual fiction, what is the real world?

Here is the real world: we cannot entrust our children's lives to our contemporary culture. That much is obvious. It is far better to entrust our culture to our children and to give them the tools to understand the forces that are unleashed to inform them, manipulate them, sell them. The intelligence of a whole person, the integrated human being, has the possibility of applying learned skills in a fast-changing world where tomorrow looks nothing like today, where fact and fiction weave through each other, driven by advertising dollars and product placement. Given a chance, our children can transform the culture before they are swallowed by it.

Everything Is Food for the Mind

The medium is the message.
— Marshall McLuhan

O ur culture glibly tells our kids to "Just Say No" to drugs and then say "Yes" to the ultra violence of television and movies, the commercialism of an over-sexualized fantasy world, and the insistence that happiness and materialism are identical. The intrusion of this unsustainable and destructive culture-mind into the psyche of our children is every bit as destructive as the drugs we have scapegoated. Everything we consume in any way is a drug—it changes the way our mind apprehends reality. Everything is food for the mind.

What is the change that takes place in an eight-year-old who watches the images of one person killing another? How about one person killing hundreds? Has the mind been altered? Has the brain been damaged? Why is this valued by society and rewarded when other brain altering substances or activities are punished?

Violent images projected through commerce-driven media literally change the brain chemistry of the child, creating both the reflection of those images in nightmares and mental agitation, and their expression in more violent behavior. This is a drug; it changes the state of mind, and there are side effects.

What is the change that takes place in an eight-year-old who eats junk food as if it were nutritious? Has the mind been altered by the onslaught of sugar, salt, fat, and chemical additives? Is there a difference between consuming carefully grown and prepared food or assembly line food-like creations? Has the mind of the child been changed by a throwaway world of styrofoam and cardboard that wraps around the meal?

How about those flickering florescent lights in the school, the pallid light of the TV and the computer screen, the microradiation of the electronic world we inhabit? How about the pressure of time, accomplishment, and acquisition we place on this same child? How about the psychological rampages parents go on with each other or the divorces when they get tired of fighting? Have we created any change in brain chemistry yet?

Let's feed a continuous stream of information and maintain a high level of mental activity all the time. Let's reward technological, financial, sports and media achievement. Let's ignore everything else. How's that little brain doing?

Let's not forget to do drug education. "Just say No." "D.A.R.E. to be drug free." We'll reward the kids by sending them off to the ball game at Coors Field or Busch Stadium.

Are the kids a little too active at school? A little amphetamine should help. Are the kids depressed at school? There are drugs for that, too. These are good drugs. Not bad drugs. Unless you don't have a prescription.

The whole of the environment is a drug. It is all food for the mind. We are, indeed, what we eat.

Sharing Our Disbelief

The mixture that is not shaken soon stagnates.

—Heraclitus

I f we believe in a market driven world, we can easily believe in preparing our children for entering that market. They are as much a commodity as anything else in that world, and they might as well be the best commodity they can be. Excellence will be rewarded by greater market share. If we believe.

We don't believe what we read in the newspapers and magazines. We certainly don't believe the network news programs. The information that makes it into these outlets has been spun so much it makes us dizzy. We know that those favored by the media are the best liars or well-connected, the ones crucified are either bad liars, guilty, or both.

We don't believe the scientists any more. We remember when we did. They promised us a rational world based on research and objective reality. They told us that fat in the diet was bad. Then they decided that some fat was good, so there was good fat and bad fat. Now they are sending up trial balloons on the problems with low-fat diets.

Scientists argue a lot. They change their minds constantly. We suspect that they are not quite as rational and objective as they say. Some even believe in God.

We used to believe in our doctors. But now medicine increasingly becomes an expression of for-profit corporate interests, and we know that those Harvard MBAs who are running the HMOs didn't do a lot of course work in compassion. Plus, the doctors have suddenly decided that there is no medical basis for circumcision—that really hurts.

Meanwhile, to bolster sagging incomes for doctors (some of which are actually sinking below six figures), medical schools are cutting back on admissions. Countering this attack on their bottom line profits, health care providers are replacing doctors with physician assistants, replacing physician assistants with nurses, replacing nurses with orderlies, and replacing orderlies with letting the patients push themselves around on those carts and empty their own bed pans.

> *A doctor, a nurse, and an HMO administrator were waiting in line to get into Heaven.*
>
> *First, the doctor spoke with St. Peter, explaining that he had done all he could to help those who were sick. St. Peter welcomed him to Heaven.*
>
> *Then the nurse said that she had done everything she could to help the doctor in his care for patients. She was given her place in Heaven.*
>
> *Finally, the HMO administrator made his case, saying that he was just following the American way of doing business, looking for the greatest efficiencies and watching the bottom line. St. Peter thought it over for a minute, and then said, "All right, you can enter Heaven, but you can only stay for three days."*

Now we have the business model beginning to be applied to the public schools, where the words *education* and *efficiency* are used in relationship to each other as if they are inextricably linked.

The word *privatization* is used instead of the more descriptive phrase, "potential transfer of billions of dollars of public money into private corporations." The pundits of profits view the schools as factories and the education of children as a product to be streamlined, measured, and priced for the marketplace like so many pork belly futures. Edu-corporations are taking over failing schools and using preprogrammed curricula that teach to the test, regardless of the interest of the child or the teacher, to create results that mean more contracts and more profit. Other corporations are creating Internet education that predigests and delivers information with religious fervor, spoon-feeding the child from five to eighteen years old with exactly what they should be learning, along with cheery virtual congratulations when they learn and the gift of relationship skills that amount to knowing how to boot up a computer. Still other companies provide free televisions with cables attached all the way back to corporate headquarters, where educational programming can be piped into the classroom for free. By the way, there will be edu-advertising, marketing products that your kids would want to know about anyway.

All these companies are fighting for just a piece of the multibillion-dollar educational market. Nickelodeon and Disney vie for the minds of toddlers, who watch more television than any other age group. Channel One, Edison, and other edu-entrepreneurs go for the kids in school. The future, no doubt, is the same as what has occurred in the educational textbook market—consolidation, as one corporation buys the other until an oligarchy controls the education of our children. This will be done efficiently and profitably. It will appear to raise the achievement levels of the students because it will raise their test scores, one way or another. And test scores, we have been convinced, tell us how our children are doing. At least, that is what the corporations that run the educational testing services would have us believe.

The great institutions of our culture—the pillars of our collective belief in our purpose and meaning: education, science, medicine, the press—are under tremendous pressure from the relentless drive for profit and efficiency. Perhaps, in the end, this is what we are left to believe in: profit and efficiency. It has, after all, brought us the best of all possible material worlds.

If we believe.

But we don't.

We know that the flow of news must cover all perspectives, science must be an open exploration, medicine is for healing as an expression of compassion, and education is the loving placement of wisdom into the hands of the generation growing up and isn't necessarily efficient or profitable. Efficiency and profit—the proceeds from commerce—support these cultural enterprises, but are not what drives them. We know that, don't we? Why then have our institutions come to reflect what we don't believe in, rather than what we know embodies a fuller consideration of our lives and each other?

Perhaps we can step back into our lives and allow them to be a little less efficient, less profitable, less material in focus. Perhaps we can prepare the way for the children who are growing up, so that their children will see a world so fundamentally different from ours that they will not believe that such a fragmented world ever sought to be. We can share with them in their disbelief.

The Heart of Learning

Don't Trust Anyone over Three

*A preschooler's tacit knowledge of grammar is more
sophisticated than the thickest style manual or the most state-
of-the-art computer language system.*

—*Steven Pinker*

Anyone who has been around young children knows that this
is the age of relentless inquiry. The world is fresh at three, if
somewhat sociopathic. The big questions are simple at this age
and they all boil down to one simple query: "Why?"

As adults around these little question machines, we often see
our job as supplying answers to these questions. This role of
holder-of-all-the-answers is soon made absurd by questions for
which we can find no answers, exasperation with seemingly endless curiosity, and the pressure we start to feel to actually get something done.

"Take your socks off, please."

"Why?"

"Because they are wet."

"Why?"

"Because you stepped in a puddle."

"Why?"

"Because you wanted to."

"Why?"

"Take your socks off, now."

And, of course, it goes on all day, every day like this.

We often mistake this behavior of the three-year-old for that of someone looking for answers. We have usually forgotten what this state of profound curiosity is really about. As adults, we inhabit a concrete world of relative certainty, and we assume that this is what the child is looking for.

This is why you shouldn't trust anyone over three.

Young children are simply curious. Learning something doesn't fulfill their interest. This thirst cannot be quenched by answers. They want to know more, regardless of what they have found out so far. Their question in life *is* their life.

We can't answer their question.

We can, however, join them in their question. That would require us to abandon all our answers. We might lose track of time. We might not get anything done today. There may be no point to the question at all. The whole thing may be totally pointless, like a game without a score, without a conclusion, without a ... winner.

Maybe it's time to get some structured play going, with rules and some competition; after all, that is what these kids are going to face in life. Why do they want to spend so much time just playing?

Or, we could teach them that there is an answer to most questions and when there is no answer, then it is time to do something else besides ask these incessant questions. Over time, we can teach them to wonder less, to give up their questioning more easily, and to accept answers as conclusions, and then they will be well prepared to go to school. After school, they can live a productive life. And we can get back to what we were doing, which is no doubt pretty important.

And what if this questioning was cultivated, not quenched? What is the potential of a child whose curiosity knows no bounds?

What would become of us as parents? What would become of our answers? What would become of our world?

We seem apprehensive of our children and their relentless drive to discover, their unfettered energy and clear eyes. Have we lost this quality so completely in our lives that we have forgotten its value? Will the world we have constructed withstand their gaze?

If we do not give our lives over to this drive for discovery in our children and in ourselves, if we restrict our children to the answers we have already formulated, it leaves us with one simple question.

Why?

To address this question in our own being we can undergo an experiment. It is helpful to get a good night's sleep before proceeding with this. Contact a friend who has a young child or, better, several young children. (If you have your own children you can skip this experiment—you've already got your own going on. Just go for the good night's sleep.) Spend a full day with the child or children, not as an adult caretaker, but as a playmate. Play without conditions. Play when you take a snack break and a lunch.

Just play.

Everything in your environment is part of the game. There is no world outside of the immediate environment. There are no complicated relationships. There are no bills to pay. There is just play.

Do you find this free-form fun exhilarating, exhausting, or both? Do you tend to form rules? Do you look for meaning in the play? Do you want to accomplish something? When your play day is over, what is your state of mind? What does your adult world look like? What does the child's world look like? Try this for an hour or for a day. If you are really serious, then try it for the rest of your life. Ask yourself "Why?" Don't answer the question. Don't stop asking the question.

The Profound Knowledge of Not Knowing

The chief cause of problems is solutions.
—*Milton Berle*

When Socrates was faced with the challenge of who amongst his peers had come to the most profound knowledge, he blew away the competition with this irony: Socrates said that his was the greatest knowledge, because his knowledge was that he did not know.

We now study Socrates as one of history's spectacular minds, while most of his philosophical contemporaries have receded into a dim history, their once grand insights now just the subject of obscure philosophy courses.

Socrates' perception was a profound understanding of the nature of learning that led him to communicate through dialogue and to discourse using the medium of questions. As one of the greatest teachers of all time, Socrates suggested that there was nothing to teach and nothing to learn, and that the knowledge of life was inherently present in each person. The question simply revealed what was already known.

In Socrates' time, teachers—known as Sophists—gathered students by means of impressive promises of knowledge and elaborate philosophies—for a fee. Teachers were paid only if the students stayed, so the Sophists generally gave long-winded, self-assured discourses using reason to prove just about anything. Their legacy is the term *sophistry,* meaning deceptive reasoning, and their shadow still falls on education today.

Socrates, in yet another expression of his greatness, refused all fees for his teaching and continued to challenge the veracity and integrity of sophistry. He was eventually put to death for his outspokenness, sending a clear signal to everyone else that those in power would rather not deal with too many questions.

Thousands of years later, Socrates' questions and death still resonate through our cultural milieu. Today, our educational institutions have largely forgotten the importance of the question and have supported new and complex forms of sophistry. Those in power have continued to make clear that questions are not in favor.

And while few would suggest that public education is not failing, fewer still would point to the suppression of the question as the causative factor. The debate continues between vouchers and general funding, between teaching fundamental curricula and teaching broad-based curricula, between outcome-based education and esteem-based education. But all this debate is within the realm of sophistry, amongst those who promise knowledge as a result of their elaborate philosophies, and whose power—and income—is based on their position in the debate.

What if they are all wrong? What if the problem with education is that it is in the way of the question? What if there is no such thing as "too many questions?" What if Socrates was right?

If Socrates was right, then the question is the teacher, school, and textbook. The whole structure of educational institutions is missing the point. There is no need to teach when there is a need to learn; there is no need for answers when there are real questions. In a question-based education there can be no curriculum, no course work, and no tests, because a question is open-ended, unformatted, and without boundaries.

A question is alive; an answer is not. Perhaps this is why schools are failing. They are full of answers. Questions fitting those answers are encouraged, tested, and rewarded. Questions not fitting those answers are disciplined, drugged, or expelled.

Public education was designed to put skilled labor into the workplace. Asking questions does not keep the assembly line moving, so education taught skills, not creativity. Industry once required such labor, but now it is less clear that this kind of worker is needed. Computers and automation continue to eliminate repetitive jobs that require only noncritical thinking. What industry is beginning to notice is that it lacks creative labor: decision makers, designers, innovators. And it is no wonder that this is the case, since public education is still functioning on principles based on its founding in the Industrial Revolution. We are in the Information Age, hurtling towards what is next. Ages are being compressed in time. Where the Industrial Age was a few hundred years, the Information Age may be measured in decades. Machines now are the heart of industry and are clearly better at storing and sorting information. There is a small window of time in which creative intelligence is still an area of human dominance, but it is just a matter of time before machines acquire complex understanding and responses superior to our own. Machines are faster; synapses are simply slower.

Then what is the purpose of education in the face of this imminent obsolescence of human intelligence? We continue to teach information when that game is already over. That is because education has nothing else it knows how to do. Education itself is obsolete but is ignorant of that fact. It needs to be educated.

Meanwhile, the creativity, the exploration, the inquiry of our young are, like Socrates, being metaphorically executed by the powerful structures of our societal paradigm for asking too many questions.

Socrates might suggest a question: "Does anything need to be done to educate the question already residing in a child?"

Spirituality and Learning

We have all been schooled to have no inner life at all.
— *John Gatto*

We have accepted the indoctrination of cultural constructs as education and, more than that, we fear that if our children miss this enculturation they will have a miserable life. Whether it is the "Great Books" of the now out-of-fashion Liberal Arts education or the math/science obsession of the brave new techno world, a specific curriculum is a modeling of what the educated person should be and, more importantly, how that person will function in society.

The parent fears for their child and so gives the child over to these forces of homogeny and social cohesion. The price is the loss of the creative and passionate expression of the child (which is un-learned through the child's education). What is purchased is security. We fear that if we do not enroll our children in this behavior modification programming, then they will face hardship and failure. They will stick out. They will not have the skills or discipline to fit in, be productive, be employed, and so forth. Failed children mean we have failed. This is what our parents feared. And their parents.

By living our own lives (of which children are an integral part) with tremendous passion, we face our fear rather than pass it on to the next generation, and we begin to put into place social forms that reflect a life of love and inquiry: intentional living communities; student-directed schools; cooperative, entrepreneurial, sustainable businesses; ecologically sound food production; relationship-based charity; artistic and media expressions that reflect more than materialism. Such a life is full of books and computers, paintbrushes and musical instruments, mystics and visionaries, along with entrepreneurs, artisans, scientists, and scholars. How could a child not be educated in a family, in a community, where life is fully lived?

While home schooling may address my child's needs, it does not address the larger question of meeting every child's needs. Home schooling may be necessary for the well being of my child because there is no alternative, but the possibility always exists of creating that alternative, for my child and for every child.

Pragmatically, the world is as it is, not as we might describe it in its ideal. We face a different kind of challenge in making sure that our life, which may be full of educational riches, is a shared life. The learning community extends our personal resources into the community at large so that any child who cares to can access the education they choose. The focus of a learning community is on a school center because our communities are not mature enough to provide a more natural, free-flowing, and integrated unschooling. Perhaps this was the ideal of public education, but not public education as it is.

The practical expression of the spiritual realization that life is interconnected is expressed in the forms we create, the work in progress of that understanding. Even a learning center that embodies freedom and responsibility is not complete until it seamlessly interfaces with the community of families, businesses, and institutions that surround it, as well as the world at large. Learning may finally be deinstitutionalized and returned to its natural state: curiosity-driven, lifelong, and incorporating every dimension of the human being.

All of this is theoretical unless we are actively living it, demonstrating it, and infusing all of what we say into all of what we live. The experiment of life may require a certain kind of refined space, but it must also be porous and interactive with the world at large. Without that openness, the experiment becomes stale and self-involved. Without doubt, we can create a bubble world for ourselves and those close to us, especially the children, but that is neither community nor educational, in the holistic sense. A closed alternative world is just the shadow side of the mainstream culture, and is part and parcel of it. The life of inquiry, the life of open learning, requires the investigation of and contact with everything, just as it is.

We all have the capacity to be still in the midst of the ten thousand forms, simply because all forms are, in fact, connected—not through those myriad forms, but through our common consciousness. Rather than try to sort the forms for the ones that please and avoid the ones that do not, is it possible for our simple awareness to move through the forms of our life, bringing with it whatever change or integration is necessary? Who is willing to step from the virtual world of safe spirituality into the life of passionate inquiry and pragmatic application of an experimental life? This is the challenge, not only for our children, but also for each of us, and all of life.

Mentoring the Heart of Learning

It is, in fact, nothing short of a miracle that the modern methods of instruction have not yet entirely strangled the holy curiosity of inquiry; for this delicate little plant, aside from stimulation, stands mainly in need of freedom; without this, it goes to wreck and ruin without fail. It is a very grave mistake to think that the enjoyment of seeing and searching can be promoted by means of coercion and a sense of duty. To the contrary, I believe it would be possible to rob even a healthy beast of prey of its voraciousness, if it were possible, with the aid of a whip, to force the beast to devour continuously, even when not hungry, especially if the food handed out under such coercion were to be selected accordingly.

—Albert Einstein

Whole education is not just the child learning from adults; it is the child learning from children, the child teaching adults, learning center staff teaching the parents, the parents teaching the staff. Children have the creativity; they are just gathering wisdom. Adults have too often lost their creativity and given up living their wisdom. Learning occurs from all directions and in all dimensions of our being, intellect, emotion, and spirit.

It is not that a child doesn't have something to learn from adults, but how that learning takes place is critical. It is practically enough if adults don't destroy the child; the rest is the child's to discover. If learning takes place through coercion, then what is learned is power, and the destruction has happened.

We cannot remove the difficulties of being a human being from anyone. Each human being has the existential challenge of what their life and life itself is about. Is it fundamentally materialistic? Is life just about getting all the possessions one can? No one can answer the question of your life for you. Each person, each child—and let us not forget that a child is a person—has to answer that question, then live the answer, then question the answer. There will be children in any environment who will answer that question, "Yes, I want the most things I can get." That is their exploration, just as it would be if they saw their life informed by other values.

An inherent intelligence comes into play in children as they are sorting through their learning process, making choices, and failing, or perhaps succeeding. Given freedom, won't they also be free to ask for help in their investigation if they need it? Won't they turn to those who are experts, who have mastered an area of knowledge?

A mentor, a master craftsman, an artist, or a researcher can teach in entirely different manners. The passionate practitioner teaches by exuding the joy in and dedication to what is loved. Now the learner can say, "I'm interested in this particular technology, craft, or area of knowledge, and you have some keys to it. I'd like to learn that; how do I go about learning this skill?"

This is the beginning of the dialogic absorption of knowledge that incidentally bears wisdom with it. The creation of relationship with the knowledge holder, the communication of a need to know, the negotiation of a social contract, and the fulfillment of the agreements and disciplines of that apprenticeship are essential aspects of the fabric of education.

Those involved set the conditions on how knowledge is going to transfer. I might say, "I'd like to show up every Monday at noon and learn violin." And you say, "Well, fine, you can do that, but you have to practice five hours a week, because I don't want to take my time to teach you violin if you're not going to practice." We have an agreement. Now, I learn from you until I have discovered what I need from the experience. This is a vastly different experience for teacher and learner than, "It's time for you to learn violin because I learned violin when I was seven, and it's good for you, and it helps your math skills."

When you meet a master in an area and you're interested in that area, you automatically give yourself over to that master, because you understand that he or she knows something. Whether it is a craft, an intellectual pursuit, or a body of expertise, a certain understanding takes place in creating and taking responsibility for the relationship to the mentor and the learning. That is an external discipline, but it comes from an inner drive and understanding that I want what this person embodies.

How does this apply to the discipline needed to learn a sport, a musical instrument, or a craft? Here, the discipline comes in the relationship between the apprentice and the master. The synergy between the deep interest of the learner and the master's love of the craft generates that discipline. Where these elements are present, discipline is the natural structure that occurs by agreement. The need to learn brings about passion, dedication, and concentration, and that creates the relationship to the master. If a student goes without those elements to a true master, that master is not going to spend the time, because the student isn't ready, isn't impassioned, isn't focused, doesn't understand their own need for that knowledge.

The master, of course, must be a true master and not a charlatan. The master must live in the joy of his craft, his art, his science. He must recognize the passion of the student as the other pole that cocreates the electricity of learning. This is not a power relationship, but a transmission relationship in which human knowledge, skill, and wisdom are passed like an endless flame from generation to generation. No one owns this flame, no one created it, and no one controls it.

Transmission may take place through an individual, through a book, through an experience. It could be music or it could be a sunset; it could be anything, because it has to do with the inner and the outer matching up, and a kind of electricity flowing through that changes me from what I was to what I am. Now I am the keeper of this flame, always ready to pass it on when the context presents itself. We are all masters and students, wizards and apprentices, when we live in the joy of learning.

If there's a passion in you to learn something, and if you have the ability to seek out resources without hindrance, then what is going to stop you from finding the master or the mentor? If that master or mentor understands the difference between indoctrination and learning, then you'll learn. This is what true masters do: they teach you what they know, and then they kick you out.

"That's it. You've got everything I know—go!" They don't let you stay in the same relationship structure. You can't fully know what you learned until you are out of their shadow and, ultimately, until you are conveying what you have learned to another.

Any learning environment has to give access to knowledge and then to give access to the door. One of the basic errors of most schools is that they give access to the information and give access to the information and give access to the information, but there's no way out, no metaphoric door. Children may learn, but they seldom have the space to experiment with that information and integrate it into knowledge and wisdom.

Mentorship teaches the fundamentals, but also allows the breakthrough. Breakthroughs come from those people who dared to step out of the known. Too often, education becomes limited to the transplanting of information rather than the spark of creativity that uses information as a tool. The mentor conveys what is already known, but must be open to what is next and to conveying this mystery. Fundamentals are learned quickly when there is an interest, and any learning environment can be set up so that fundamentals can be accessed at any point where they will actually be useful to the learner.

In the absence of a mentor, then the free learner naturally takes the role of a scientist, experimenting to find that mastery, investigating through books what others have done, interacting with other students who share the enthusiasm. Perhaps other students have a passion for chess, trigonometry, lost-wax sculpture, or Chinese poetry.

A learning community is a crossroads to a broad range of mentors. If I want to be a drummer, a writer, an engineer, or a bricklayer, there is a mentor who will work with a group of motivated students, and there are students who will communicate their desire to learn and their responsibility for the rigors of the process. Of course, if I want to learn bricklaying on my own, I can experiment with a pile of bricks and some mortar. I may make a crooked wall, but I will learn something about experimentation and about learning.

Together, those who are interested may organize a class. We may even organize it in a traditional fashion, finding a teacher, perhaps even a lecturer, a demanding and unforgiving disciplinarian. But it will be our passion that meets the demand of the teacher and makes the learning happen. It is our interest that transforms this seemingly traditional didactic form into something that is vital and magical.

The mentor need not be a magician, but need only understand that interest in learning. The skill of the mentor lies in allowing the learner to discover that passion and the learning that is its constant companion.

Creating Learning Communities

The Living School

A free dialogue may well be one of the most effective ways of investigating the crisis which faces society, and, indeed, the whole of human nature and consciousness today. Moreover, it may turn out that such a form of free exchange of ideas and information is of fundamental relevance for transforming culture and freeing it of destructive misinformation, so that creativity can be liberated.

— *David Bohm*

Instead of accepting the increasing centralization of education and the corporate and governmental intrusions that characterize the education of our day, why don't we insist on keeping not just our schools in the immediate community, but our children as well?

Children don't really need to go to a specific place to learn. They learn wherever they are, whether in a home or in a community. This home and community—the collection of all homes, workplaces, businesses, and public facilities—could be their school. All that is missing are the parents and the other members of the community making their homes into something more than a place to eat and sleep, and making their communities into expressions of relationships rather than just activity. All that is needed, in other words, is a simple thing: the total remaking of our society, its values, and its structures.

This should be no problem, really. We have the motivation. We love our children and want the best for them. And most of us wouldn't mind being fulfilled ourselves.

To teach our children to innovate, to create, and to actualize, we must do the same. We can look at each aspect of our lives to see if it represents the expression of the human potential rather than the habit of security. We can organize learning communities, not just for our children, but for all of us: living schools that move and flex with the challenges of our lives and needs. We can recognize the need to integrate our society, not just in terms of race, sex, or class, but also to integrate the various age groups from infant to elder, so that the fullness of the human experience can be shared. We can expand our sense of our lives to include more than just me and mine, to touch you and yours, to merge the facets of each of our lives into a jewel of all of our lives.

Productivity and Happiness

Has nature, then, made a monumental error in creating a child who compulsively spends most of his or her time in apparently nonproductive and even antisurvival activities of fantasy, magical thinking, and play?
—*Joseph Chilton Pearce*

We are well trained in our roles and in our obligations to our children. It is not surprising then that we send our children off every day to learn how to live in this same way. It certainly would not come naturally to them to go on their own, nor is it likely we would send them off without being taught to do so.

We could not get to the life that we are living without going through an education system that prepared us by destroying our creativity. Children are not naturally going to live an emotionally shutdown life. They are already in touch with something that is alive, unfettered, and unafraid. But this energy of the child has very little to do with the ability to produce the goods and services that a society considers important. If cars can be built on an assembly line then students can be educated on an assembly line. Our society worships the efficiency of the assembly line, its automation, its relentless production; it is a god that must be appeased, or it will stop providing.

Every once in a while, we begin to wonder about the life we have come to live; we wake up in the middle of the night questioning our meaning and fulfillment. It is disturbing when we realize that assembly lines, cubicle farms, and cyber serfdom don't have happiness built into them, like one more benefit along with the 401K and medical plan. These forms were engineered for productivity, not well-being.

We hear our own voice like we are channeling ourselves from another dimension: "Well, it's time to send the kids off on that little school bus. Bye, kids. Now, where was I? Oh, yes, I'm going to work now, because it's time to be productive. That question, 'Am I happy, are they happy, are we happy?' will have to wait, because I'm really quite busy."

Industry knows it needs to produce happiness in its workers; it cuts down on absenteeism, turnover, and sick days, if nothing else. Our highly productive society is plagued by school and work-place violence, epidemic levels of depression and hyperactivity, divorce, domestic violence, child abuse. Armies of consultants offer advice on how to create the appearance that we are in relation-ship in our highly productive society. We have the illusion of con-tact and the "reality" of television, where we experience people competing to "survive" while the helicopter hovers around film-ing them. By the millions, we believe that's relationship.

The workplace now has counselors who are helping people relate to each other. And if that doesn't work, there are, of course, the mind-altering substances that keep us happy whether we're happy or not. And if we're not happy, we don't care, because it's a little hard to get through all those layers of chemicals to say *what* we are. But it doesn't make a difference, because it's time to go to work, time to put the kids on the school bus; we're busy. That's our world as we have created it.

Is there an alternative to that world? What is the something else that we could do? Or is that just the way it is? The sun rises in the east and it sets in the west. That's the way it is. The school bus comes, the kids get on, we go to work. That's the way it is, that's the way it has to be.

Is there any other possibility? If I don't put the kids on the school bus, it's a problem. Now they're home, and I've got to go to work. What if I don't go to work? That's a problem. Landlord or lender comes knocking on the door. Now I'm homeless, I've got the kids, what do I do? This is the result that fear projects if we step into the unknown and begin to create another possibility. But, is this fear accurate?

Is there a different basis from which we can function? Could we cooperate with each other? Could fewer of us go to work and some of us care for the kids? Or could we work together? Could we work cooperatively? Could we create businesses together? Could we have the businesses at home? Could you envision a world in which people actually lived and worked together, and kids lived with them, learned with them, worked with them? Is that imaginable?

Don't just look at productivity as the measure of life. Consider integration, helpfulness, and happiness in the assessment. Look at the whole, sustainable system, including generations to come. Take into account the cost of productivity, efficiency, and profit in terms of human happiness. We cannot just look at a nuclear plant as something that can produce cheap electricity. Now we have to look at what it costs to decommission a plant. What does it cost if one of them melts down? Can we look at the whole picture?

What happens when we begin to approach life in a new way? Fear may occur because we haven't been here before. We know what the world has been, and now we are considering a world we don't know. We can't really get a sample of it from our past. We have to step into it first, and that is terrifying.

In our life, is fear or curiosity predominant? Is the need to explore the unknown greater than the need for security? We have to face that question every day: when we go to work, when we put our kids on the school bus, when we live what we already know is failing us and failing the world around us. When we approach this question of a vital life and an integral education, we're approaching the question of our own fear.

The fear of the unknown is the limitation on our creativity, the essential expression of our happiness and that of our children.

Can we produce an alternative learning environment without going deeply into this question of what we do with our life?

Can our life be a mechanical process and yet produce a school that is different? Can we send our kids to a place where they will be free if we're not free? Can we produce a place where kids can be unbound if our homes, our society, and our world are not? Or does the whole of it have to shift?

We can produce a school where kids decide for themselves what they're learning, a school that is run democratically rather than hierarchically, with innovative, experiential learning, without artificial segregation of children by their skills or their age. But the question of education goes deeper than just structures of a school.

Doesn't that school have to connect to lives that also embody the same qualities? Doesn't that school have to touch parents who are willing to live their lives in an integral way? Doesn't it have to touch other kinds of institutions working toward a different model of family, society, workplace, and social organization? If we're not demonstrating this possibility through our lives, we cannot expect our children to live it. How can they possibly learn in a new way if we are not living in a new way?

What holds the space of total change and revolution in human consciousness? It seems unlikely that we could create a space that is whole within a space that is fragmented. Our passionate interest in and love for our children and for all children can catalyze a new, fearless approach to our lives and learning. We can create a learning environment that is not designed to implant a certain way of experiencing the world, but allows children to learn in freedom what the world actually is. A child who learns in that way may well transform the world, but, at the very least, that child will live unfettered by our fear.

The Intentional Family

Ours was a house for children, rather than a real school. We had prepared a place for children where a diffused culture could be assimilated without any direct instruction.
—Maria Montessori

The breakdown of the family structure has been blamed for many of the social problems of our society. In contemporary reality, the family is often broken, marriages end in divorce as frequently as they don't, and parents remarry, blending pieces of families into new families. With the rapid changes in society and the increased mobility of life, the intergenerational biological family is often stretched in geography and time beyond its capacity to function as a supportive unit. There is little doubt that these changes in social organization add stress to the lives of children. It is also, quite possibly, an opportunity to reconsider the family, to create new structures, not of biology, but of mutual intention, relatedness, and familiarity.

It is a worthy experiment to create a new kind of family, a supportive grouping of children and adults who live in close proximity to each other, even in intimacy, and who, through their commitment and shared perspective, formulate a life that has all the closeness and utility of a family. The nuclear family functions well for some, but not for all. And, for many, the breakdown of a marriage means a life of single parenting; for children, it can mean a lack of resources, attention, and security.

Could a household be made up of single parents committed to supporting and raising their children? Could a cohousing community be made of those who support each other in the fabric of a day-to-day life? Could individuals make covenants of commitment that transcend the historic forms of marriage? Could a piece of land or a building hold a number of children and adults (married and single) who are de facto aunts and uncles, nieces and nephews, parents, grandparents, and children—family in everything except biology?

Is the biological imperative so strong that we cannot see relationship in each other unless we share our genes? We make an exception in order to marry another, but that is perhaps to procreate. We make an exception in order to adopt, but often that is because procreation failed. Is the demand of biology that we organize around the selfish gene? Or is the selfish gene intelligent in its requirements? Won't our children be better off in an intentional family if a biological family is not available, or perhaps as a supplement to a traditional marriage? Aren't we better off with others to share the burdens of life, to help and be helped by, living in the familiarity of commonality?

Is the cultural paradigm and the pressure to maintain the traditional status quo too intense to allow the possibility of a healthy reconfiguration of family-like groupings? Is this too odd, too eccentric, too threatening? What is the taboo against mutual care and concern, and why could it not be fashioned in new ways?

We do not need to accept the alternative to family that currently presents itself in our culture: isolation, loneliness, and the virtual relationship of telephones, email, and hurried visits by airplane. We can seek out others who share our vision for an integrated life, communicate what we and our children need, and listen closely to the response. We can cocreate intentional families of any size, with any combination of adults and children, of any generational structure and share what is most important in our lives—our care, our support, and the nurturing of all the best that is the expression of the human potential.

With a stable family structure, whether it is traditional, intentional, or both, our children will be rewarded with more time, attention, care, and love. By attending to our deepest aspirations and giving expression to them in our intimate relationships, we will give our children a family that is carefully chosen and constructed for their well-being. And in the intentional family, in whatever form it takes, we can have the foundation for an intentional life, a life that blossoms with creativity and curiosity and is a vital component of a society of families that constitutes a learning community.

Living Communities

Perhaps it is the specter that most haunts working men and women: the planned obsolescence of people that is of a piece with the planned obsolescence of the things they make.
— *Studs Terkel*

In the same way that families have been fragmented by contemporary society, the very structure of our communities has changed. In an overloaded, overstimulated, and overwhelming world, community structures often reflect the desire for privacy, safety, and control. While these are components of social satisfaction, our culture has turned into a disconnected world of isolation.

We can live for years next to a neighbor we have never met. The physical space of our suburban housing allows us to drive in and be engulfed by an interior world that only we know. Our view of the outside is through our television or a window looking onto our backyard privacy fence. In the suburbs, we drive everywhere. Walking is for the occasions when the dog needs exercise or when the shopping center parking lot is so crowded that we have to park in the outer lot. In urban areas, safety, noise, and pollution aggravate our lives. Our life is so given over to productivity, mobility, and speed that the community is just a place for us to be alone, to rest, and recover for another day and another dollar.

This life is designed to divide, and it is not what we want. We have begun to create cohousing communities that give individual privacy but also create the structure of connection. Suburbs have started embracing neotraditional designs for front porches and cross streets, pocket parks and walking trails. Urban areas are creating mixed-use projects and live-work space, reclaiming the energy of the town center. Cars are yielding ever so slightly to alternative modes of transportation that are not only ecologically sound, but community friendly. Even the virtual world of the Internet has spawned cybercommunities that transcend time and space and connect those with common interests.

At the cutting edge of this movement toward connection-based living are those who see the importance of the quality of life, the value of relationship, expression, receptivity, appreciation, affection, and kindness. These qualities cannot be commodified, marketed, and sold, although many have tried. They are components of a life of consideration, of passion, of inquiry. They occur naturally, at no cost other than the abandonment of our obsession with materialism.

Our children are at ease with these aspects of a related life, and once we were too. But we have come to believe we must work hard at our spirituality or our therapy to regain our access. This is unfortunately just more of the same effort, the same perspective of acquisition and materialism, the security of spiritual narcissism that never looks beyond its own needs.

In fact, we need do nothing to regain the paradise of a life of connection other than to recognize it all around us: the acquaintance we never took time to get to know, the cup of tea we never stopped long enough to savor, the novel we never finished, the help we never gave, the conflict we never resolved, or the journey we never took. There is not more to do to discover the life of passion; rather, less doing is needed from our busy minds, and more from the spontaneity of our hearts in each moment of our lives where, in the end, relationship is discovered.

As we reawaken to the life of connection, we will need structures that reflect the considered pacing and profound intensity of that life. Our community becomes the expression of that restructuring; not a community in which we live, but a community as a medium through which we live. This community, our community, reflects and expresses the most profound elements of the human potential.

The living community is wherever we are, whether this is the intentional community of a cohousing project or the cul-de-sac, no-exit, existentialist limbo of suburbia, whether a communal household or the worst of urban-isolation, fortress architecture. It is the recognition that if I am fully alive, then everything I connect to can be infused with that vitality.

The living community, the electricity that crackles through all social structures, is the ground of commonality; it is the shared space of a life that embraces us all, and that we recognize as holding the potential for greater integration, creativity, and compassion. This connection to our community is our lifeblood, because it is our life. It is where our lives and our children's lives take place. To separate from it is to separate from ourselves, to hold back from our own fullness.

Our children need more than a home and a family, essential as those components are. They need a community out of which they will emerge into the world at large and to which they will return again and again, perhaps to stay and live, perhaps to simply share their life and leave again. A child needs a community, not a place of anonymous houses and strip malls, but a living community. This is more than a place. It is all the potentials of relationship located in a place. Such a community is alive: where the structures of society support the inquisitive, the creative, the passionate; where roads lead not just to destinations but to discovery; where houses are built not just to protect but to connect; where productivity, creativity, living, and learning are not divided by architecture and zoning, but integrated into forms that reflect the deepest aspirations of the human being.

Our children need a community that embraces them, advises them, mentors them, shows them skills, and gives them knowledge. And our children need a community that asks for their cooperation, requires their responsibility, and accepts their help, energy, and creativity.

We cannot protect our children from a world gone mad by cocooning in our isolated homes any more than we can protect them from our increasingly poisonous food supply by restricting them from eating. Children crave community just as they crave food. Junk food and soda may seem like food. Television and the Internet may seem like community. Perhaps they will get by with these facsimiles, but why don't we make it our life business to feed them from our gardens and connect them to a living community?

Life is as it is, and while we may call it a mad, mad world or a wonderful life, it is still just as it is. We cannot protect our children from what is. Reality will always present itself despite our efforts to escape it. But the world, as it is, is not static. Life is alchemical; change happens. Transformation is potential in every moment. We can hold the still wisdom of perceiving life as it is and, at the same time, feel the immense urgency of transforming it into a world of ever-deepening connection. If we engage our community fully with such love and vigor, we can create a world that is habitable for our children and for all children, a community that embraces us back. We have breathed life into it, and now it is a living community.

Learning Communities

It is the great triumph of compulsory government monopoly mass-schooling that among even the best of my fellow teachers, and among even the best of my students' parents, only a small number can imagine a different way to do things.
— *John Gatto*

When our communities start living, then we have the potential of non-localized learning. These are communities where life, work, play, and education are integrated. The school is an anachronism in such a community, a form that no longer functions in an age of seamless information and experience.

The learning community is a society that accepts as part of its function the education of its young and the continual need of its adults to learn. In a learning community, there is no distinction between learning and living. This community understands that learning information in isolation from experience is pointless, that a child who cannot innovate has not learned a basic life skill, and that learning connected to the actual life that we live is dramatically more potent than the rote learning of the typical school environment. The learning community knows that all of its participants will need to access lifelong learning in order to move through the multiple careers that have become the norm; indeed, to embrace even one career fully requires continuous learning. In a deeper sense, the community that holds the vision of itself as an integrated learning process understands the vital essence of the human experience: if learning is not part of everything we touch, then our life is not fully actualized.

Businesses, which have to be nimble to be successful, may sense this need more than any other institution in our society. While the large corporations are often encumbered by outmoded and amoral structures referencing the past, the most agile of them understands that a corporate culture that learns is vital. The corporate world and the academic world are so interconnected in flow of funds and personnel that it is often difficult to distinguish their boundaries. While this can lead to corruption when funding overdirects research, it also provides a model of how immensely useful it is to integrate learning and productivity. Further, large companies find that the team building that results from employees volunteering for community service enhances productivity.

Business is discovering, much to its surprise, that it pays to break down the barriers that have been erected between home and work, between work and community, and between work and schools. It pays because people are happy when they are connected, and work that comes from a happy person is less problematic and more creative. It is not so difficult to envision the possibility of happiness being the point of productivity. The learning community is the community that lives, works, and learns together, and brings innovation, creativity, and efficiency to that productivity as an expression of happiness.

Learning communities are simply the stringing together of libraries and museums, homes and workplaces, universities and schools of all kinds, hospitals, research facilities, and government agencies into a constantly evolving learning space. A student could access what is needed, design independent study, and learn through contracts, apprenticeship, or even employment in a vast array of facilities with an enormous range of mentors. This school without walls would not simply emulate the structures of life, but would be the life that we share, with each other, with our children, with our elders. The learning community is the intergenerational passion for learning that doesn't begin or end in childhood, or even in a particular lifetime, but that makes up all of life.

For the child to access this educational continuum, he or she would need the responsibility that freedom requires, the direction that curiosity gives, and the effort that self-direction naturally expresses. Where these qualities were lacking in a child, perhaps schools would have a function as remedial facilities where children could relearn their natural state of interest and refocus their direction. Schools could be social and resource centers. Schools could be practically anything useful, except what they tend to be today: places where children learn to stop learning and to obey, memorize, and repeat.

For the teacher, the role of disciplinarian and didact falls away. The teacher, upon discovering his or her own deep interest in learning, ceases to teach and begins to demonstrate, transmit, and inspire. The teacher becomes an example of a life of learning, available to share with others of all ages what has already been discovered and what is now being investigated.

In a reversal of the old mocking adage of "those who can, do; those who can't, teach," the new teacher, the happy teacher, is a doer who loves what she does and teaches through example. This is, of course, what teachers in our current system of education want as well: the freedom to learn, the responsibility to chart their own course, and the chance to teach learners who come to them in the joy of discovery. The happy teacher, like the happy child, makes all the difference in the educational equation. The destruction of this natural impulse to convey wisdom turns the teacher into a mechanical presence in our schools, every bit as repressed as the children they once sought to help. The learning community is the liberation of teachers as much as it is the liberation of children.

The parents in the learning community have the extraordinary chance to share their lives with their children, not just in the tired hours of the evening or the occasional activities of the weekend, but as part and parcel of a daily life. The mystery of the disappearing parent who goes off to some unknown place to something called work is solved. The learning community, where the parent goes to work and learn, is part of the same community where the child goes to learn, and is where, in the end, they all live. The community is commonality of place, purpose, and relationship. The parent is the creator of this place and invites the child to join in that creation. Together, they live a life, seamless in its construction, where the point is happiness and the place for its expression is where they work, learn, play—and live.

All adults function as parents in a learning community. They understand that whether they have children of their own or not, nothing is more important in a society than the care of the young. The richness that makes up a happy life doesn't come from the accumulation of pleasures and possessions, but from the relationship with all those who share that life. In the learning community, in freedom and responsibility, and in the expression of creativity and inquiry, we are all beneficiaries of the whole and, in our individual expressions, the creators of it as well.

Is this what makes our life full and content, kind and creative, fulfilled, happy? It is not just the child who needs these qualities, but each of us in relationship to all of us: learning, helping, and loving. Our children are simply profound reminders that changing the heart of education means opening our own hearts, not just to our children, but also to each other.

About the Author

Steven Harrison is the author of *The Question to Life's Answers, Being One, Doing Nothing* and *Getting to Where You Are.* He is a founder of All Together Now International, a charitable organization that aids street children and the destitute in South Asia. He is also a founder of The Living School, a learning community in Boulder, Colorado, where he lives.

Those interested may write:

Steven Harrison
P O Box 6071
Boulder, CO 80306
InDialog@aol.com
www.doingnothing.com

For more information:

The Living School
P O Box 6105
Boulder, CO 80306
Email: contact@LivingSchool.org
www.LivingSchool.org

Sentient Publications, LLC publishes books on cultural creativity, experimental education, transformative spirituality, holistic health, new science, ecology, and other topics, approached from an integral viewpoint. Our authors are intensely interested in exploring the nature of life from fresh perspectives, addressing life's great questions, and fostering the full expression of the human potential. Sentient Publications' books arise from the spirit of inquiry and the richness of the inherent dialogue between writer and reader.

Our Culture Tools series is designed to give social catalyzers and cultural entrepreneurs the essential information, technology, and inspiration to forge a sustainable, creative, and compassionate world.

We are very interested in hearing from our readers. To direct suggestions or comments to us, or to be added to our mailing list, please contact:

SENTIENT PUBLICATIONS, LLC
1113 Spruce Street
Boulder, CO 80302
303-443-2188
contact@sentientpublications.com
www.sentientpublications.com